A Brief Account of the Finances and Paper Money of the Revolutionary War.

BY J. W. SCHUCKERS.

SANFORD J. DURST
Numismatic Publications
New York, N.Y.

Sanford J. Durst
133 E. 58th Street
New York, N.Y. 10022 U.S.A.

Library of Congress Number 77-74029
ISBN 0-915262-12-6

Originally published by
John Campbell & Son
Philadelphia
1874

This volume has been published in a limited edition of 500 copies

This is copy No. 252

This book has been produced with an attractive, quality, durable cover. It is the opinion of the publisher that paper dust jackets are ecologically wasteful, and for that reason are not provided.

THE WRITER'S PREFACE.

I DO not pretend, in this little volume, to any new discoveries touching the financial history of the Revolutionary War, but only to having brought together, in one place, those facts which are of prime interest and importance. They are written down with almost statistical brevity, but he who thoughtfully reads them will see how painfully our forefathers struggled and suffered to bring us "out of the land of Egypt, out of the house of bondage."

Ours is the only great nation which, in the Nineteenth Century, has paid a public debt contracted for war purposes, and it is not the least of the proud achievements of the American people. I have brought my little book to an abrupt close, because I wished to say *here* what might perhaps have been more appropriately said in a closing paragraph. It is this: That the most glorious celebration we could have have made of our Centennial Anniversary, would have been the simple announcement that, for a second time, in the first century of our national existence, we had paid off a public debt. To do this would have required great exertions and great sacrifices, but such exertions and sacrifices were not beyond the powers of the American people.

I will be allowed to add that the surest and safest way to a resumption of specie payments is through the extinction of the public debt. Its payment ought to be the paramount object of every administration, and is a policy commended alike by National Duty and National Honour.

J. W. SCHUCKERS.

New York, October 1st, 1874.

THE REVOLUTIONARY FINANCES.

I.

Paper Money—technically called Bills of Credit—were issued by the colony of Massachusetts Bay certainly as early as 1690; and probably some years previously bills were emitted by private persons upon the security of private properties. There is evidence that in 1686 a bank was formed in that colony by a gentleman of Boston, with several others, some from England, who were authorized to begin the issuing of bills on the security of real and personal estates; but we have so little record of its history that no detailed or definite account of it can be offered. We learn from the Massachusetts Archives that authority was given to seven persons to start a bank and issue bills, in these words: "And having perused and considered a proposall made to us by John Blackwell, of Boston, Esqr., on behalf of himself and divers others, his participants, as well in England as in this countrey," liberty is granted to the directors or "conservatives" of the bank to commence the issuing of bills on real and personal security, and on merchandise. The writer of a pamphlet, entitled "A Letter from one in Boston to his Friend in the Country, in Answer to a Letter directed to John Burrill, Esqre., 1714," says: "Our fathers about twenty-eight years ago entered into a partnership to circulate their notes, founded on land security, stamped on paper as our Province bills now are."[1]

2. Bills of credit were issued by the several colonies prior to the revolutionary war, and for their payment the public faith was pledged. They were called in by taxes payable at different periods, and were not only made receivable in payment of taxes, and of all debts due to the government making them, but were made a tender also in payment of private debts, until this was prohibited by Act of Parliament in 1763. Massachusetts led the way in making and issuing this species of money. That colony incurred expenses in an unfortunate maritime expedition against Quebec in 1690, much beyond its ordinary means of payment, and to meet these expenses resorted to the expedient of issuing bills of credit of the colony. This was afterwards followed, as cases of emergency arose, by most if not all the other British North American colonies. They became less valuable, however, in every colony in which they were issued, than gold and silver. In New England they were valued at six shillings for a silver dollar, and at that rate were denominated the lawful money of that part of the country; in New York they were valued at eight shillings, and in Pennsylvania at seven shillings and sixpence for a dollar; and hence arose the different currencies in the several colonies. Excessive emissions caused depreciations. In

---

[1] NATHANIEL PAINE: "Essay on Early Continental Currency."

1745 Massachusetts alone—to pay the expenses of her fortunate expedition against Louisbourg, and in other preparations in the war then existing between France and England—emitted bills to the amount of between two and three million pounds lawful money. This large increase in the amount of bills in circulation naturally occasioned a greater depreciation, so that in 1748 eleven hundred pounds of these bills were only equal to one hundred pounds sterling.[1]

3. Governor POWNALL gives this account of the Pennsylvania system: "I will venture to say there never was a wiser or a better measure, never one better calculated to serve the uses of an increasing country, that there never was a measure more steadily or more faithfully pursued, for forty years together, than the loan office in Pennsylvania, formed and administered by the Assembly of that province." He gives a sketch of the loan office act passed in the year 1739, which he styles "the completest system of the kind, containing all the improvements which experience had from time to time suggested in the execution of the preceding acts. By this act the trustees of the loan office were to lend out the bills on real security of at least double the value for a term of sixteen years, to be repaid in yearly quotas or instalments with interest. Thus one-sixteenth part of the principal was yearly paid back into the office, which made the payments easy to the borrower. The interest was applied to public services; the principal during the

[1] TIMOTHY PILKIN: "Statistical View of the Commerce of the United States."

first ten years was let out again to fresh borrowers. The new borrowers from year to year were to have the money for only the remaining part of the term of sixteen years, repaying by fewer and proportionately larger instalments, and during the last six years of the sixteen the sums paid in were not to be reloaned, but the notes burned and destroyed; so that at the end of the sixteen years the whole might be called in and burned, and the accounts completely settled. The trustees of the loan offices were taken from all the counties of the province; their residence in different parts of the state giving them better opportunities for being acquainted with the value and circumstances of estates offered in mortgage. They were four years continued in office, accounted annually to committees of the Assembly, and at the expiration of that term they were to deliver up all moneys and securities in their hands to their successors before their bondsmen could be discharged."

Various methods prevailed in the different colonies for issuing bills, but the Pennsylvania system was generally considered the best and safest; the paper was made a legal tender in the payment of debts, and generally maintained its original value, with slight fluctuations, caused by a rise in gold and silver when a larger quantity of these metals than usual was wanted for exportation.[1]

4. In the modern mode of making war, money is not less essential than valour in the field or wisdom in the cabinet. The deepest purse decides the fate of nations as often as the longest sword. It early occurred

---

[1] SPARKS: "Life of Franklin."

to the founders of the American empire, that the established revenues of Great Britain must eventually overbalance the sudden and impetuous sallies of men contending for freedom, on the spur of the occasion, and without the permanent means of defence; but how to remedy the evil puzzled their wisest politicians. Gold and silver, so far as was known, had not a physical existence in the country in any quantity equal to the demands of war, nor could they be procured from abroad, as the channels of commerce had been previously shut by the voluntary association of Congress to suspend foreign trade. America having never been much taxed in any direct way, and being without established governments, and especially as she was contending against what was lately lawful authority, could not immediately proceed to taxation. Besides, as the contest was on the subject of taxation, the laying on of taxes adequate to the exigencies of war, even though it had been practicable, would have been impolitic. The only plausible expedient remaining in their power to adopt was the emission of bills of credit representing specie, under a public engagement to ultimately sink them in taxes or exchange them for gold or silver.[1]

5. PELATIAH WEBSTER, who wrote a series of Essays during and subsequent to the war, which were full of wisdom, and plethoric with italics,—a man well acquainted with the resources and financial condition of the colonists,—says the current cash just before the war was commonly estimated at about $30,000,000, though the real sum did not probably exceed

[1] RAMSAY: "History of the American Revolution."

$12,000,000—of which about $5,000,000 was gold and silver.[1] Colonial bills formed the chief part of the circulating medium.

---

[1] LORD SHEFFIELD—"Observations on the Commerce of America"—estimated the specie in the colonies prior to 1775 at about $9,000,000; BLODGETT ("Manual") at about four millions. This latter is no doubt much nearest the truth.—(Both cited in SEYBERT'S *Statistics.*)

II.

WHEN, therefore, the SECOND CONTINENTAL CONGRESS —an immortal body!—addressed itself to a consideration of the finances, almost immediately upon its meeting, May 10th 1775, nothing was more natural and probable than a prompt resort to paper money. First, it provided for the creation of an army. Having done this, and entirely conscious that the supply of cash—(cash is a good word: a better than either specie or coin, though the latter has a ringing sound, cash being defined by JOHNSON to be "money; properly *ready* money; money in the chest or at hand;" a good thing to have and a sure friend);—the members of the Congress being entirely aware, then, that the supply of cash was inadequate even for the current and ordinary business of the colonists, immediately betook themselves to BILLS OF CREDIT, of which on the 22d of June they ordered an emission of two millions of dollars; and in July another emission of one million. Two joint treasurers[1] were appointed as custodians of

[1] The original administrators or custodians of the funds of the Continental Congress were two joint-treasurers, appointed July 29th 1775; subsequently, August 6th 1776, one of these resigned, and one only was continued in office. In February 1776, a committee of Congress, five in number, was appointed to superintend the treasury; and in July 1779, a Board of Treasury was constituted; its principal officers consisted of five commissioners, two of whom were members of Congress and three were not; its duties were, the general management of the

these and other funds of Congress,—and they were authorized and directed, whenever they should have gold and silver in their hands for the redemption of the bills, to advertise the fact; thereby signifying that they were ready to pay it to such holders as desired an exchange. HENRY PHILLIPS says he has made diligent search—as perhaps some bill-holders did during the war—for an advertisement of the treasurers, and found none! No doubt. However, the Congress, proceeding apparently upon the belief—and perhaps they did believe—that gold and silver could be procured for at any rate partial conversions, and also to provide funds for the ultimate redemption and sinking of the bills, made an estimate of the supposed population of the colonies, including therein both negroes and mu-

---

finances of the United States, the preparation of estimates of expenditures, the auditing of accounts and the like. But this Board of Treasury was found to be an exceedingly cumbrous and inefficient body, and gave way, in February 1781, to a *Superintendent of Finance*—ROBERT MORRIS—whose duties were substantially those exercised by the five commissioners, and more extensive in some important particulars, as will hereafter appear. On the retirement of Mr. MORRIS, 1784, a Board of Treasury was re-established; this time consisting, however, of but three members, and its powers included those of the Superintendent also. The Treasury Department of the United States was organized under the Act of Congress of 2d September 1789; next to the President, the principal officer of this department is the most important personage in the government, though technically outranked by the Secretary of State. He digests and prepares plans for the improvement and management of the revenue and for the support of public credit; prepares and reports estimates of the public revenues and the public expenditures; collects the revenue, and grants, in the way prescribed by law, all warrants for moneys paid out of the treasury; is the only member of the Cabinet who makes annual reports directly to Congress; he appoints a multitude of subordinates, and exercises large and varied powers generally in connection with his office.

lattoes, and allotted taxes among them in proportions based upon that estimate: the bills to be received in payment of the taxes (which were of course to be laid by the local assemblies of the states, the Congress having no authority to do any such thing), and the receipts into the state treasuries to be paid into the continental treasury in four yearly instalments, the first to become due in November 1779; it being the expectation that long before the period arrived for the first payment the war would be ended. Exclusive of slaves at the South the estimate of population was this: New Hampshire, 200,000; Massachusetts, 352,000; Rhode Island, 58,000; Connecticut, 202,000; New York, 238,000; New Jersey, 138,000; Pennsylvania, 341,000; Delaware, 37,000; Maryland, 174,000; Virginia, 300,000; North Carolina, 181,000; South Carolina, 93,000; Georgia (unrepresented at the date of this estimate), 27,000: total, 2,243,000. Add 500,000 slaves, and the ultimate was 2,743,000. It was upon the basis of this estimate that all the taxes and expenses of the war were distributed among the states; it was conjectural, of course, and although some of the states complained that it was unequal, and Congress recommended them to take efficient means to arrive at a correct knowledge of the numbers of their inhabitants, no enumeration was made. In 1782, however, the authorities of New Hampshire caused a census of the state to be taken, and found the actual population to be but 82,000 souls.

The bills authorized in June did not get into circulation until August. They were received by the public with great favour. They circulated at the par of gold;

"that the endangered liberties of America ought to be defended, and that the credit of their paper was essential to a proper defence," were the opinions engraven on the hearts of a great majority of the people. It was a point of honour, and was considered as a part of duty, to take the bills freely at their full value. While the ministry of England were puzzling themselves for new taxes and funds on which to raise their supplies, Congress raised theirs by resolution."[1]

On the 29th of November following—estimates having been made of the expenses already incurred, and of those probable to accrue up to the 10th of June 1776, "in the defence of America," Congress resolved upon a further emission of three millions, upon the same plan as of the issues authorized in June and July. In calculating the estimates to June 1776, Congress proceeded upon the expectation then prevailing, that by that time a reconciliation would be effected with the Crown, which, as the reader is entirely aware, did not happen.

---

[1] Ramsay.

III.

February 17th, May 9th and 27th, July 22d, August 13th, November 2d, and December 28th 1776, additional emissions were ordered; the aggregate for the year being nineteen millions, and the whole emissions to the 1st of January 1777, were twenty-five millions. "The United States for a considerable time derived as much benefit from this paper creation of their own, though without any established funds for its support or redemption, as would have resulted to them from the free gift of as many Mexican dollars. But there was a point both in time and quantity beyond which this congressional alchemy ceased to operate. That time was about eighteen months from the date of their first issue, and that quantity about twenty millions of dollars."[1]

2. But long before the expiration of the year, Congress began to realize the importance of some other means of financial supply than continued emissions of paper dollars. Though the bills were not actually depreciated, they began to be seriously discredited at a period not long subsequent to the "Declaration of Independence." That act had wrought a radical change in the objects of the war, and was certain indefinitely to prolong it, and just as certain indefinitely to increase

---

[1] Ramsay.

the expenditures. It began to be widely apprehended that the cost of liberty is something more than vigi-.ance; it is a considerable percentage of the income of the people. A good many whigs, even in those days of patriotism and sacrifice, were almost as anxious about their pocket-books as they were about their liberties, and realized—as men in these degenerate days do—that liberty without money is like a nobleman without an estate,—the mere shadow of a lord. They received the bills with some reluctance, and paid them out as promptly as was consistent with a respectable regard for the cause. Gold and silver disappeared, and prices advanced, which is but another way of saying that the circulation is superabundant, or is in bad credit, or both. "The stock of hard money which we possessed in an ample degree at the beginning of the war, soon flowed into Europe for supplies of arms, ammunition, and other necessaries, which we were not in the habit of manufacturing for ourselves. The produce of our soil, attempted to be carried in our own bottoms to Europe, fell—two-thirds of it—into the hands of our enemies, who were masters of the sea; the other third illy sufficed to procure the necessary implements of war, so that no returns of money supplied the place of that which had gone off. A paper medium completed the exile of the hard money; in the later stages of the war we were, for years together, without seeing a single coin of the precious metals in circulation."[1] Contractors were multiplying, and those persons who

[1] Thomas Jefferson.

do all sorts of chores for the public and are paid in commissions, were far more numerous in Revolutionary days than now; seeing that almost the whole purchases of supplies for the armies were made upon commission, and the percentages allowed were more than liberal—they were extravagant. "What shall I say," asked a curious and indignant observer, in a communication to one of the newspapers,[1] "what shall I say of the commissions allowed to quartermasters and commissaries, with their hosts of deputies? I am far from impeaching every man who handles public money, but look into every county in this and the neighbouring states, and see the change in the manners of the deputies in the staff departments. Come with me to a public sale. The man of ancient patrimonial estate is outbid for everything by an assistant-deputy quartermaster's clerk! See him lay down *his*—I retract the word—*your* tens of thousands for a farm. There is no end to his purchases. And unless you put an end to the amazing perquisites of your staff officers"—many of whom, the writer alleged, were taken out of the billiard-rooms—"I expect in a few years to see the delegates in Congress tenants of their own quartermasters and commissaries!" Briefly, then, resuming our narrative, the more sagacious began clearly to forecast the future, and to prepare for it. But,—

3. Congress dealt with these people as summarily as they knew how, or as they had power to deal with

---

[1] "Pennsylvania Packet."

them, for in those days states' rights were things and not words; in very truth the states had so many rights they did not know exactly what to do with them all; still they preferred keeping to delegating them, and suffered countless present ills rather than submit to others that might be worse: so Congress, limited, and one might say almost shackled, could only indulge a sort of political excommunication—not upon admitted authority, however—but a very powerful and effective kind of excommunication after all. "Any person who shall hereafter be so lost to all virtue and regard for his country as to refuse the bills or obstruct and discourage their currency or circulation, shall be deemed, published and treated as an enemy of the country, and precluded from all trade and intercourse with its inhabitants."[1] Concerning which we shall see more hereafter.

4. Congress had no power to tax; but seeing that something had to be done besides emitting bills and excommunicating infidels who did not believe them the equal of cash, a loan was proposed [October 3d 1776] of five millions of dollars. This was no interference with the rights of the states—a beggar may borrow if any one be willing to lend. Interest at four per cent. per annum was offered, and for the convenience of lenders, loan offices were to be established in the several colonies, to be in the charge and keeping of commissioners selected by the local authorities, for Congress did not feel authorized to designate even such officers. The commissioners were to have one-

---

[1] Resolution of Congress, January 11th 1776.

eighth of one per cent. upon the whole sums brought into their respective offices, in lieu of all other claims and demands for transacting the loan business; not a very lucrative compensation, seeing how small the receipts were and the money seriously depreciated. This was the beginning of the loan-office system. The certificates of loans were to be of the denominations of three hundred, four hundred, five hundred, six hundred and one thousand dollars; and Congress, with a characteristic attention to details, directed not only the devices which were to be engraved upon them but also the colours in which they were to be printed. Gouverneur Morris alleges that these certificates on their first appearance were in less repute than the bills of credit, "for causes not necessary to be mentioned, as they are fresh in everybody's memory."[1] It was hoped and expected by Congress that as the certificates bore interest they would absorb the bills and be hoarded. The result was otherwise. Being made payable to bearer, they were not only transferable but actually were transferred from hand to hand, and instead of checking or diminishing the depreciation, largely contributed to promote it.

5. Lotteries in the revolutionary age were not in the disrepute which attaches to them in this generation; and even if they had been, it is quite likely Congress would have resorted to one if it had promised any considerable results. At any rate a scheme of much magnitude was framed, and a good deal of time and attention were devoted to it. It dragged its slow

---

[1] "Pennsylvania Packet." April 11th 1781.

length along through several years, and was substantially a failure, though a good many people, ambitious of sudden and accidental fortune, bought tickets. The lottery certificates were among the transferable securities of the times.

6. The states separately emitted large quantities of bills of credit. As they swelled the volume of the circulation, and were in as good repute—being based upon substantially the same security—as the continental bills, they were potent in hurrying on the discredit and then the depreciation of the whole mass of the currency. Against these emissions Congress, in future years, appealed fervently and vainly. Though the state assemblies had power to tax, taxes were unpopular; and if there is anything in the world an American legislator holds in abhorrence, it is personal or political unpopularity. So the states didn't tax, but they printed with unflagging vigour. Private persons, seeing the mania for paper money, issued circulating notes; and some of these were quite as good and some of them were a good deal better than the bills either of the state governments or of Congress, but they were prohibited under severe penalties. The counterfeiters were active, and their issues became a wide-spread and formidable evil. The English government—which seems to have a mania for counterfeiting the paper money of its enemies—entered into competition with private criminals in this highly civilized way of carrying on the war.

7. In this place it may be as well to advert to the probable amount of the issues of the states. It is impossible accurately to state their amount; THOMAS

JEFFERSON estimated them at two hundred millions, an estimate which the table in the appendix shows to be very near the truth; and the circulating value of the state bills was, in general, neither greater nor less than that of the Continental emissions.

8. The whole issues of Congress, from June 1775 to January 1st 1777, aggregated twenty-five millions of dollars, and their purchasing power, during the campaigns of '75 and '76, was equivalent to that of specie, though, in consequence of the great abundance of paper, prices had steadily advanced.

IV.

THE beginning of 1777 found the bills at an open discount of not less than one hundred per cent. Notwithstanding the declaration of Congress, that "they ought to pass current in all payments and dealings, and be deemed equal in value to the Spanish-milled dollars," their credit was steadily downward. "The continental money," said the resolutions of Congress on the subject (dated January 14th 1777), "ought to be supported at the full value expressed in the respective bills, by the people of the states, who stand bound to redeem them according to the like value, and also to guard against the artifices of the enemies of liberty, who impair the credit of the bills *by raising the nominal value of gold and silver.*" At the same time, as a remedy for the depreciation, the state legislatures were recommended to pass laws inflicting penalties and forfeitures upon persons who sold their land sand merchandises for continental bills *rated at a specie value*, and to make them *a lawful tender* in the payment of both public and private debts; debts payable in sterling money to be discharged with continental dollars at 4*s.* 6*d.* sterling per dollar (that is to say, at par), and in discharge of all other debts and contracts to pass as the equivalent of the Spanish milled dollar, a refusal of the bills at these alleged values to operate as an extinguishment of the debt. To these appeals the states responded, with what effect will be hereafter seen.

2. The campaign of 1777 was conducted with paper money, and was not seriously affected by its decreased and fluctuating value. At the beginning of the year two paper dollars were equal to one hard dollar, and in December one hard dollar was worth four paper ones. The emissions authorized in the mean time were thirteen millions, worth at a cash valuation about three millions. A great quantity of counterfeits were put into circulation; this evil became so great that it was found necessary at a later period officially to withdraw from circulation two of the continental emissions, amounting in the aggregate to ten millions of dollars.

3. Congress, with an earnestness almost pathetic, appealed to the legislatures not only to refrain from further local issues of bills, but to call in and cancel those already emitted; they were urged to take measures for the limitation of prices, and to authorize the seizure of supplies in the hands of forestallers and engrossers and pay for them at fixed rates, and to tax their people. Taxes to the amount of five millions, to be raised during the year 1778, were allotted among the states: New Hampshire was called upon for $200,000; Rhode Island for $100,000; Massachusetts, $820,000; Connecticut, $600,000; New York, $200,000; New Jersey, $270,000; Pennsylvania, $620,000; Delaware, $60,000; Maryland, $520,000; North Carolina, $250,000; South Carolina, $500,000; Georgia, $60,000. Hitherto, said the address of Congress to the legislatures, "we have not burdened our

fellow-citizens with taxes, but have raised the necessary supplies on the public faith; and the same method has been embraced by the respective states to answer their internal wants. The currency is by these expedients multiplied beyond good policy, and its comparative value is proportionately reduced. To this cause, conspiring with the arts of open and secret enemies—the shameful avidity of professed friends and scarcity of foreign commodities—are we to ascribe the depreciation of our currency. The consequences to be apprehended are equally obvious and alarming; they tend to the depravity of morals, the decay of public virtue, a precarious supply for the war, debasement of the public faith, injustice to individuals, and the destruction of the honour, safety and independence of the United States." Hitherto spared from taxes, the people were now called upon, "with cheerful hearts to contribute according to their circumstances." But the sums set down against the respective states were not to be considered as their real proportions, but being paid into the common treasury were to be placed to their credit, and interest allowed at the rate of six per centum per annum.

4. Signal advantages—so Congress said—having been derived from the establishment of the continental loan offices, it was recommended, at the same time, that the system be further extended by the opening of subscriptions in all the towns, counties and districts of the several states.

V.

SEEING with extreme and just alarm the public and extensive depreciation of the currency, Congress and the people, at the beginning of 1777, cast about for prompt and efficient remedies. We have already seen the declaration of Congress in January 1776, that persons refusing the bills should be treated as public enemies, and that at the period of which we are now writing penal laws were recommended against those who made a discrimination against the continental currency. Excommunication not having been sufficiently effective, it was now determined to proceed to punishment.

2. "The fatal error that the credit and currency of the continental money could be kept up and supported by acts of compulsion, entered so deep into the mind of Congress and of all departments of administration through the states, that no considerations of justice, religion or policy, or even experience of its utter inefficacy, could eradicate it; it seemed to be a kind of obstinate delirium, totally deaf to every argument drawn from justice and right, from its natural tendency and mischief, from common sense and even common safety. Congress began, as early as 11th January 1776, to hold up and recommend that maxim of maniaism, when continental money was but five months old. Congress then resolved that whoever should refuse to receive in payment the continental bills, should be

deemed and treated as an enemy of his country, and be precluded from all trade and intercourse with the inhabitants; *i. e.* should be outlawed—which is the severest penalty (except life and limb) known to our laws. This ruinous principle continued in practice for five successive years, and appeared in all shapes and forms, in tender acts, in limitations of prices, in awful and threatening declarations, in penal laws with dreadful and ruinous punishments, and in every other way that could be devised; and all executed with a relentless severity by the highest authorities then in being, to wit: by Congress, by assemblies and conventions of the states, by committees of inspection (whose powers were in those days nearly sovereign), and even by military force; and though men of all descriptions stood trembling before this monster without daring to lift a hand against it, yet its unrestrained energy was ever found ineffectual to its purposes, but in every instance increased the evils it was designed to remedy, and destroyed the benefits it was intended to promote; at best its utmost effect was like that of water sprinkled upon a blacksmith's forge, which indeed deadens the flame, but never fails to increase the heat and force of the internal fire. Many thousand families, of full and easy fortunes, were ruined by these fatal measures, and lie in ruins to this day, without the least benefit to the country, or to the great cause in which we were then engaged."[1] But others, perhaps as competent to judge, thought the tender and limitation laws the efficient instruments that saved the country. And who shall say *these* were not the true prophets? Un-

---

[1] Pelatiah Webster: Essay printed in 1790.

doubtedly those laws were cruel in spirit and execution; less rigorous and distressing remedies might have been equally potent in curing the evils; we cannot say, for they were not tried, or being attempted, were found impracticable of execution. What is certain is, that while the tender and limitation acts did not and could not completely prevail against the inexorable laws of traffic, they were very powerful in their effects, and for some brief time, at any rate, preserved a degree of credit for the bills even after they were utterly valueless. Now, nothing less than this can truly be said. And when one reads the history of those disastrous and most distressful days,—when tories and savages from over the sea, as well as savages from the wilds and jungles of America, were joined together in despoiling and desolating the country, when counterfeiting and lying were added by our enemies to their swords and rifles as means of war upon our ancestors: now YOU, sitting—so to speak, but metaphorically only of course—under your own vine and fig-tree, with none to molest or make you afraid; MILL, RICARDO and AMASA WALKER (wise, all of them, in their day and generation, but none of them *there* present to partake in the calamities and griefs of the war), saying sage judicial things and impressing you with the soundness of their philosophy on the currency question,—recall the fear and distress of the people of America in those days of trial, their poverty, loss of trade, homes destroyed, fields and farms laid waste, open enemies assailing them with arms, and secret, insidious and unscrupulous enemies lying in wait for them at their very doors; recall all these surroundings of danger and difficulty, and if you be a financier,—and no doubt you are,—heaven forefend that anything here said should imply a suspicion to the contrary,—after all, what *could* have been done other than what *was* done? The fathers, driven to extremity, resorted to those measures which promised the most immediate and certain relief. The intrinsic error was in the use of paper money; for true it is that paper money being in the nature of evil, its use must ever be attended with abuse; and while nobody doubts the vast influence it has exerted in modifying the whole structure of modern society, and the powerful effective instrument it has been in the creation of material wealth, the untold suffering it has inflicted upon people of all ranks and conditions in every country in which it has been used, is not at all compensated by the good it has wrought, if indeed it has wrought any.

3. The fathers of the republic, being reduced then to the necessity of emitting paper money, notwithstanding the evils that followed in its track, were bound to use every means to support its credit. All considerations other than THE SAFETY OF THE STATE must of necessity give way. Public and private justice were sacrificed, corruption of manners, extravagance, improvidence, disgraceful habits of suspicion, espionage and cheating, were introduced among a really virtuous people.

4. The first of the pernicious system of laws which WEBSTER condemned so trenchantly were those making the bills a legal tender in payment of debts. Congress recommended the states to do this, and Rhode Island led off in August 1775 in doing it. The other states,

one by one, did the same, and all attached severe penalties for refusing the money at its nominal value. So long as the bills remained at par, but little mischief resulted; when they were in course of depreciation great evils and hardships followed. A well-known historian has described the general operation of the continuously-enlarging volume of paper, and at the same time the legal tender. The possessors of the bills, he says, who either from sagacity or accident conjectured rightly as to their ultimate fate, or finding that they daily lost a part of their value, were perpetually in quest of bargains. As they knew that Congress must make further emissions to supply the armies, they concluded that it would be better to purchase up property of any kind than to lay up their money, while the deceitful sound of large nominal sums tempted many possessors of real property to sell, some of them opulent persons of ancient family; and on the other hand, again, some hoarded up the bills in preference to buying solid property at supposed extravagant prices. Many bold speculators made fortunes by running in debt beyond their present abilities, and paid their debts in a depreciating currency; the merchants and moneyed men were great losers by the legal tender. It changed the nature of obligations so far that he was counted an honest man who on principle delayed to pay his debts. It disposed those who were losers by the legal tender, and who preferred their money to the liberties of America, to wish for a re-establishment of British government, and filled others with murmurings and bitter complaints against the ruling powers. The public-spirited, who were sincere in their declarations of devoting life and fortune to the cause of their country, patiently submitted to their hardships from a conviction that the cause of liberty required the sacrifice.[1]

All classes were infected. The paper produced a rage for speculation. The mechanic, the farmer, the lawyer, physician, members of Congress, and in some places even a few of the clergy, were contaminated. The morals of the people were corrupted beyond anything that could have been believed prior to the event. All ties of honour, blood, gratitude, humanity and justice were dissolved. Old debts were paid when the paper money was more than seventy for one. Brothers defrauded brothers, children their parents and parents their children. Widows, orphans and others were paid for money lent in specie with depreciated paper, and were compelled to receive it.[2]

That the helpless part of the community were legislatively deprived of their property was among the lesser evils which resulted from the legal tender of the depreciated bills of credit. The iniquity of the laws estranged the minds of many citizens from the habits and love of justice. The mounds which government had erected to secure the observance of honesty in the commercial intercourse of man with man were broken down. Truth, honour and justice were swept away by the overwhelming deluge of legal iniquity.[3]

The tender laws were substantially the same in all the states; and their vital principle was, that a tender

---

[1] RAMSAY: "History of South Carolina."

[2] GORDON: "History of the War of the American Revolution."

[3] RAMSAY: "History of the American Revolution."

of the bills, whether accepted or refused, equally worked an extinguishment of the debt. They were repealed in the early part of the year 1781; but to the very last, and in despite of the known misery and injustice wrought by them, they had warm and persistent advocates—they had been revised during the spring of 1780 to conform them to the "forty-for-one" scheme of Congress of March 18th of that year, though at the very moment of revision the depreciation was ten to twenty-fold in excess of the rate fixed by law; but in Maryland, and perhaps in other states, contracts to be discharged in gold and silver were made lawful, which in some measure at any rate relieved the people.

It may be observed here: it seems impossible to doubt indeed—that the framers of the constitution from personal knowledge aware of the intrinsic viciousness of legal tender paper, intended to prevent its use by constitutional prohibition.[1]

---

[1] The debate in the Federal Convention is here cited in support of this observation:

Mr. GOUVERNEUR MORRIS moved to strike out "and emit bills on the credit of the United States." If the United States had credit such bills would be unnecessary; if they had not, unjust and useless.

Mr. BUTLER seconds the motion.

Mr. MADISON: Will it not be sufficient to prohibit the making them a *tender?* This will remove the temptation to emit them with unjust views. And promissory notes in that shape may in some emergencies be best.

Mr. GOUVERNEUR MORRIS: Striking out the words will leave room still for the notes of a *responsible* minister, which will do all the good without the mischief. The moneyed interest will oppose the plan of government if paper emissions be not prohibited.

Mr. GORHAM was for striking out without inserting any prohibition. If the words stand they may suggest and lead to the measure.

5. The second of the system of laws for supporting the *value*, or more properly the purchasing power of

---

Mr. Mason had doubts on the subject. Congress, he thought, would not have the power unless it were expressed—though he had a mortal hatred to paper money, yet as he could not foresee all emergencies, he was unwilling to tie the hands of the legislature. He observed that the late war could not have been carried on had such a prohibition existed.

Mr. Gorham: The power, as far as it will be safe or necessary, is involved in that of borrowing.

Mr. Mercer was a friend to paper money, though in the present state and temper of America he should neither propose nor approve of such a measure. He was consequently opposed to a prohibition of it altogether. It will stamp suspicion on the government to deny it a discretion on this point. It was impolitic also to excite the opposition of all those who were friends to paper money. The people of property would be sure to be on the side of the plan, and it was impolitic to purchase their further attachment with the loss of the opposite class of citizens.

Mr. Ellsworth thought this a favourable moment to shut and bar the door against paper momey. The mischiefs of the various experiments which had been made were now fresh in the public mind, and had excited the disgust of all the respectable part of America. By withholding the power from the new government, more influence would be gained to it than by almost anything else. Paper money can in no case be necessary. Give the government credit and other resources will follow. The power may do harm—never good.

Mr. Randolph, notwithstanding his antipathy to paper money, could not agree to strike out the words, as he could not foresee all the occasions that might arise.

Mr. Wilson: It will have a most salutary influence on the credit of the United States to remove all possibility of paper money. This expedient can never succeed whilst its mischiefs are remembered; and as long as it can be resorted to, it will be a bar to other resources.

Mr. Butler remarked that paper was a legal tender in no country in Europe. He was urgent for disarming the government of such a power.

Mr. Mason was still averse to tying the hands of the legislature *altogether*. If there was no example in Europe, as just remarked, it might be observed, on the other side, that there was none in which the government was restrained on this head.

Mr. Reed thought the words if not struck out would be as alarming as the mark of the Beast in Revelation.

the bills, were those for the limitation of prices. The deluge—for it could be called nothing else—of paper money which flooded the country, steadily and rapidly raised the prices of commodities of every kind. The rise was attended by embarrassing fluctuations; they made the poor poorer, if they did not make the rich richer, as indeed in many cases they did. The people, feeling the pressure constantly grow greater, with the income of this week able to purchase less than with the income of the last week, and this constantly recurring, became restless, impatient, clamorous and even threatening. They were not political economists, and could not trace the trouble to its real source, but naturally enough charged it upon forestallers, engrossers and the tories. Having arrived at this conclusion—and there *were* bulls and speculators, forestallers, engrossers and "withholders" in those days—they cast about for a remedy. If prices could be kept down the trouble would be prevented,—anybody could see *that* Why not limit prices, then? This idea seems to have originated in New England; and Congress, impressed with a belief that limitations would be effective in sustaining the bills, seized upon the New England idea,

---

Mr. LANGDON had rather reject the whole plan than retain the three words, "and emit bills."

Nine states voted to *strike out;* two states to *retain.* Virginia voted in the affirmative, and in explanation of his vote with his state Mr. MADISON appends a note, thus: "The vote in the affirmative by Virginia was occasioned by the acquiescence of Mr. MADISON, who became satisfied that striking out the words would not disable the government from the use of public notes, as far as they could be safe and proper; and would only cut off the pretext for a *paper currency*, and particularly for making the bills *a tender* either for public or private debts."—See *Madison Papers*, iii. 1343, 1344, 1345, 1346.

and recommended it to the states [November 22d 1777], for their immediate adoption, and renewed it in respect of various details during the ensuing two years. Apply the regulations, said Congress in substance, to the prices of labour, to manufactures, internal produce and imported commodities,[1] to the charges of innkeepers and to land and water carriage: limit the number of retailers in the counties, and make them take out licenses to observe the laws made for their regulation; let such persons as have no licenses be restrained from purchasing greater quantities of clothing and provisions than are necessary for family use,—and upon offenders against these laws let such penalties be inflicted *as will brand them with indelible infamy!* Seize and forfeit the stores of forestallers, engrossers and withholders; seize the supplies also of any persons who have larger quantities of commodities than are competent for the private annual consumption of their families; and pay such prices as you shall think proper. The excessive spirit of sharping and extortion was to be put down most certainly. "We are convinced," said Congress in January 1779, "that there is not so much diligence used in detecting and reforming abuses as in committing and complaining of them!" And later in the same year—November—Congress declared that the fluctuating state of prices not only caused inequality and injustice in private dealings and in procuring the public supplies, but rendered it impracticable to make proper estimates for future expenses, and to fix equitably the salaries of employees of the United States; that as the estimates upon which

[1] Military stores to be excepted, however.

the requisitions for taxes upon the states were based proceeded upon the principle that the prices of commodities necessary for the public use should not exceed twenty-fold of the former prices, it was urged upon the states to enact laws for a general limitation in accordance therewith: that is to say, upon the principle of an advance of twenty-fold above the prices current through the various seasons of the year 1774. According to THOMAS JEFFERSON'S table the depreciation at the time these recommendations were made was thirty-eight for one. In order to hasten action, it was declared that those states failing to enact laws upon this principle before February 1st 1780, should be charged in the public accounts with the aggregate amount of the difference between prices paid from and after the 1st of February next in such states and those paid in states enacting the laws.

Some idea of the prevailing feeling of the people in relation to forestallers and engrossers may be gathered from the expressions of WASHINGTON on the subject. "Certain I am," he said, "that unless extortion, forestalling and other practices, which have crept in and become prevalent and injurious to the common cause, can meet with proper checks, we must inevitably sink under the load of accumulated oppression. To make and extort money in every shape that can be devised, and at the same time decry the value (of the paper money), seems to have become a mere business and epidemical disease, calling for the interposition of every good man and body of men." To President REED he wrote: "It is most devoutly to be wished that some happy expedient could be hit upon to restore the credit of our paper emissions, and punish the infamous practice of forestalling and engrossing such articles as are essentially necessary to the very existence of the army."

It was in 1779 and 1780 that the popular excitement in relation to the limitation laws and the "nefarious practices of forestallers and engrossers" was at at its wildest. Public meetings were held in the different cities and towns, and violent penalties and denunciations—in addition to the legal penalties and forfeitures provided by the states in pursuance of the recommendations of Congress—were denounced against offenders. Not only were offenders denounced; they were also punished in property and person.[1] It is enough to say—as Mr. WEBSTER truly observes—that the local committees of safety and inspection exercised almost sovereign powers. Their decrees were rigorously executed, but notwithstanding the

---

[1] "*Rid the community of the* monopolizers *and* extortioners *who, like canker worms, are gnawing upon your vitals. They are reducing the currency to waste paper by refusing to take it for many articles. We have borne with such wretches, but will bear no longer. Public* examples *are public* benefits! *You then that have articles to sell, lower your prices; you that have houses to let, refuse not the currency for rent; for, inspired with the spirit of those heroes and patriots who have struggled and bled for their country, and moved with the cries and distresses of the widow, the orphan and the necessitous,* BOSTON *shall no longer be* YOUR *place of security!*"—From a broadside poster, Boston, June 16th 1779. It contained also a caution—"*Lawyers, keep yourselves to yourselves.*" A second broadside about the same time contained these words: "THE CRISIS! Remember that the old spirit of opposition to the stamp act that first originated at Boston and sounded the alarm through the continent, is not yet smothered, but shall soon burst with an unabating vengeance on the heads of monopolizers as it did on the odious stamp masters. BY HEAVENS IT SHALL NOT DIE!"

violence and stringency of the measures of repression, the depreciation pursued its inflexible course, though doubtless measurably restrained.

6. Partaking of the character of the limitation laws were those laying embargoes upon the exportation of grains and provisions. Congress alleged that such exportations occasioned serious difficulties in procuring supplies for the army, and by the capture of exporting vessels by British ships relieved the enemy from distresses that would greatly have embarrassed his operations. Declaring it absolutely necessary, therefore, that an embargo be immediately laid, and unwilling to await the action of the state legislatures—some of them distant from Congress, and assembling at different periods—lest the purposes of the embargo should be frustrated, Congress proceeded to lay a prohibition upon the exportation of wheat, corn, beef, pork, live-stock and other provisions, and recommended the states to enforce it with the necessary regulations. This was on the 8th of June 1778, and the embargo was to continue in force till the 15th of the following November. On the 2d of September Congress so far modified the prohibition as to allow provisions to be exported from Pennsylvania and the states south of Pennsylvania to eastern ports, for the use of the people of the Eastern States, but this permission having led to fraudulent clearances, on the 2d of October the states were recommended to grant no exemptions from the general operation of the laws, unless the shipper and every seaman and passenger on the vessel should solemnly swear, without any mental reservation or equivocation, that neither directly nor indirectly were they

concerned in any measure whatever that might tend to prevent the arrival of the vessel in the eastern port of destination, and the shipper was required also to agree before departure upon the price at which the flour or grain was to be delivered. Congress continued the prohibition from time to time, and the states aided by enacting the laws necessary to carry it into execution.

VI.

Now, touching the confiscation acts[1] of the several states, it may as well be stated here as elsewhere that at various periods during the war, acts were passed by all of them to confiscate and sell, to sequester, take possession of and lease the estates of the loyalists—that is to say, of the tories—and to apply the proceeds towards the redemption of certificates and bills of credit, or towards defraying the expenses of the war; to enable debtors to pay into the state treasuries or loan offices paper money in discharge of their debts to British and tory creditors. Under some of these laws many individuals were attainted by name, others were banished for ever from the country, and if found within the state were declared felons without benefit of clergy. In some states the estates and rights of married women, of widows and minors, and of persons who had died within the territories possessed by the British arms, were forfeited. Autho-

---

[1] The operation of the confiscation and tender laws was thus described by DANIEL DULANEY, a citizen of London and a subject of the British Crown, and a *refugee*. He was the residuary legatee of ANN TASKER, who died at Annapolis, Maryland, in 1775, and the sum of ANN TASKER's property, after paying other legatees, which belonged to DANIEL DULANEY, amounted to about £14,000 sterling, chiefly in outstanding debts due the estate. DANIEL DULANEY had other property in Maryland, the whole of which, including ANN TASKER's legacy, was confiscated by act of the legislature, and sold for the benefit of the state, to the amount of

rity was given to the executive departments to require persons who adhered to the Crown to surrender themselves by a given day and abide trials for high treason; in failure of which the parties so required were attainted, were subject to and suffered all the pains, penalties and forfeitures awarded against persons convicted of high treason. In New York a power was vested in the courts to prefer bills of indictment against persons *alive or dead*, who had adhered to the king or joined his fleets or armies; if in full life and reputed to hold or claim, or if dead to have held or claimed at the time of decease, real or personal estate. And upon notice or neglect to appear and traverse the indict-

---

upwards of £70,000 current money. By public acts of the provincial convention and legislature, the executor of ANN TASKER (being the father of DANIEL DULANEY) was prohibited from bringing suits for the recovery of the debts due to her estate; but by an act passed in February 1777 bills of credit emitted by Congress and the state of Maryland were made a legal tender in payment of all debts at the rate of 4*s.* 6*d.* sterling per dollar, and a tender of such bills, whether accepted or refused by the creditor, or his or her executor or administrator, not only extinguished so much of the debt as was tendered, but the creditor refusing to deliver up the evidence of the debt to be cancelled upon demand, was thereby subject to have the same recovered upon an action of trover, together with damages for the detention. Under this act very large sums of legal tender paper money were tendered to the executor of ANN TASKER by sundry debtors of her estate, and the executor, to avoid the penalties he would have incurred under the law for refusing to receive it, as well as to escape the public ignominy and popular vengeance he would otherwise have inevitably sustained, was compelled to receive the paper at the rate of 4*s.* 6*d.* sterling for each dollar, when in fact it was worth but one-fifth of that sum; and the executor being compelled to make good to the other legatees their respective claims upon the estate of ANN TASKER, the whole loss fell upon DANIEL DULANEY, and amounted to about £10,000 sterling money of Great Britain; and DANIEL DULANEY sought to recover the real value of the debts due the estate of ANN TASKER and his other confiscated property, and succeeded in doing neither.—*MSS. in Pa. Hist. Society.*

ment, *whether in full life or deceased*, were respectively declared guilty of the offences charged and their estates forfeited, whether in possession, reversion or remainder. In some of the states confiscated property was applied to the purposes of public buildings and improvements; in others it was appropriated as rewards to individuals for military services rendered during the war, and in one instance, property mortgaged to a British creditor was liberated from the encumbrance by a special act of the legislature as a provision for the representatives of the mortgagor, who had fallen in battle. Even after the war, in some of the states, the confiscation laws were acted upon, and new regulations made to carry them into effect. The British government paid to the loyalists about seventeen millions of dollars on account of losses sustained by them in consequence of these various enactments.[1]

---

[1] See the correspondence between Mr. HAMMOND, the British Minister, and Mr. JEFFERSON, Secretary of State, during WASHINGTON's administration, touching alleged failures in carrying out certain stipulations of the Treaty of Peace between Great Britain and the United States.—AMERICAN STATE PAPERS: FOREIGN RELATIONS.

VII.

WHILE Congress was struggling at home with the embarrassments always attending upon disordered finances, the cause of America found powerful friends and extensive helps among generous foreigners.

2. Let us recount these:

The efforts of BEAUMARCHAIS to engage his government to aid the colonists began so early as 1774. His versatile talents and indefatigable zeal were not without their due effect upon the French King and his prudent Minister of Foreign Affairs; but the difficulty of assisting the colonists without compromising the peaceful relations of England and France had indisposed them to give or lend the colonists anything—but their ears. Early in 1776, however, BEAUMARCHAIS devised the commercial disguise through which the French government might give aid and comfort to the enemies of England without the risk of being treated as one of the number. His project, the history of which fills one of the most romantic pages in the chronicles of the country, received the approval of VERGENNES, and suddenly, like a shifting scene in one of his dramas, a blazing sign proclaimed that the mysteriously-begotten firm of RODRIGUEZ, HORTALING & Co. had established its headquarters in the Hotel d'Hollande, in Paris, and the author of the "Marriage of Figaro," who never did anything except in a grand way, was in less than a year the most extensive shipping-merchant in Europe. In the course of a few months, after he had brought the King to his views, several ships loaded with what the colonists most needed—cannon, mortars, shells, cannon-balls, small-arms, nearly three hundred thousand pounds of powder, and tents and clothing sufficient for 25,000 men—were despatched to the United States, to be in readiness for the approaching campaign of 1777, which was expected in England to put an end alike to the war and the callow young republic that was fighting for its existence. Before the summer of 1777, BEAUMARCHAIS was in advance for supplies to Congress nearly a million of dollars, for which he had counted upon prompt returns in tobacco and other merchantable products of the country. Unhappily the jealousy of ARTHUR LEE and the eccentricities of BEAUMARCHAIS rendered his operations completely unintelligible to Congress. "Imagine," says DE LOMINIE, in his admirable Life of BEAUMARCHAIS, "imagine serious Yankees, who had nearly all been traders before becoming soldiers, receiving cargo after cargo, which were frequently embarked by stealth during the night, and the invoices of which constantly presented some irregularities, and all this without any other letters of advice than the rather bombastic missives signed with the romantic name of RODRIGUEZ, HORTALING & Co., in which BEAUMARCHAIS mixed protestations of enthusiasm, offers of unlimited services and political advice, with applications for tobacco, indigo or salt fish, and indeed with tirades, of which we may take the following as an example: *Gentlemen,—Consider my house as the head of all operations useful to your cause in*

Europe, and myself as the most zealous partisan of your nation, the soul of your successes, and a man profoundly filled with the respectful esteem with which I have the honour to be, etc., RODRIGUEZ, HORTALING & Co.—The calculating disposition of the Yankees naturally inclined them to think that so ardent and fantastic a being,—if after all such a being really existed,—was nothing but a commercial comedy agreed upon between the French government and himself, and that they might in all security of conscience use of his supplies, read his amplifications, and dispense with sending him tobacco." Which they did. BEAUMARCHAIS received neither tobacco, nor thanks, nor even a letter from Congress. His communications remained unanswered, his funds and credit were exhausted, and all his expectations of returns were disappointed. Congress persisted in treating him as a sort of *Mrs. Harris,* whose existence was more than doubtful. At last reduced to extremities, he sent to the United States a confidential agent, to obtain, if possible, some explanation of results so chilling to his enthusiasm, and for which he was so poorly prepared. This agent made ardent efforts to effect a settlement of the claims of his principal against the republic, but ineffectually, and it was not until long after the members of the Congress he had assisted, and BEAUMARCHAIS himself, had gone "where the wicked cease from troubling and the weary are at rest," that his heirs obtained a final settlement with our government.[1] BEAU-

[1] See "Beaumarchais, the Merchant," a lecture delivered by JOHN BIGELOW before the Historical Society of New York, and printed by SCRIBNER 1871, from which this account of BEAUMARCHAIS is extracted.

MARCHAIS'S claim against the United States amounted to 4,547,593 livres, approximating to one million of dollars. A deduction of one million livres was made, and the remainder was paid; and in 1835 his heirs were allowed by the Congress of the United States a further sum of eight hundred thousand francs.

3. Besides the assistance received through BEAUMARCHAIS, the French government paid to the American commissioners in Paris, previous to the treaty of 1778, two millions of livres as a gratuity, and the Farmers-General of France loaned them a million.

The aids received from France from the beginning to the end of the war, besides men and ships, are these: Previous to 1778, and including the loan of the Farmers-General, 3,000,000 livres; in 1778 loan 3,000,000 livres; in 1779 loan 1,000,000 livres; in 1780 loan 4,000,000 livres; in 1781 loan 4,000,000 livres; subsidy 6,000,000 livres; loan in Holland guaranteed by France 10,000,000 livres (5,000,000 Dutch florins); in 1782 loan 6,000,000 livres; and in 1783 loan 6,000,000 livres.[1] That is to say, the

[1] The six million livres borrowed in 1783 were advanced from the royal treasury to "answer numerous urgent and indispensable expenses in the course of the year." The contract made between the King of France and the United States, on the 25th of February, contains these words: "The Minister Plenipotentiary of the United States having represented to the King the exhausted state to which the Americans have been reduced by a long and disastrous war, His Majesty has taken into consideration the request of the American Minister, in the name of the Congress of the United States, for a new advance of money to answer numerous urgent and indispensable expenses in the course of the present year, and notwithstanding the no less pressing necessities of his own service, has determined to grant to Congress a new pecuniary assistance, which he has fixed at the sum of six million livres tournois, under the title of loan under the guarantee of the whole thirteen United States."—See *Journal of Congress for* 1783.

French government assisted the United States to the extent of 43,000,000 livres; 9,000,000 in the way of subsidy, 24,000,000 by loans, and 10,000,000 by guaranty—total, $7,962,962. The French loans carried interest at the rate of five per cent. per annum; the Dutch loan four per cent.; as to that on the French loans, "His Majesty being willing to give to the United States a new proof of his affection and friendship, makes a present of and forgives the whole arrears of interest to the day of the treaty of peace, a favour which the Minister of the Congress of the United States acknowledges to flow from the pure bounty of the King."[1]

---

[1] See the third article in the contract between the United States and France, completed at Versailles July 16th 1782.

VIII.

On the 6th of February 1778 Louis XVI. entered into treaties of amity and commerce and of alliance with the United States, on a footing of the most perfect equality and reciprocity. By the latter of these the French King became the guarantee of their sovereignty, independence and commerce. The Marquis de Lafayette was among the first in the American army who received the welcome tidings. In a transport of joy he embraced General Washington, exclaiming—"The King, my master, has acknowledged your independence, and entered into an alliance with you for its establishment." The joy felt by the people and the army exceeds description. The several brigades assembled by order of the Commander-in-Chief, and offered public thanks to Almighty God. "Long live the King of France!" burst from the breast of every private in the army. The Americans fancied that peace was within view. But Congress was wiser, and that the people might not be lulled into a dangerous confidence warned them: "You must yet expect a severe conflict; though a foreign alliance may secure our independence, it cannot save our country from devastation."[1]

And so the event proved.

---

[1] Ramsay.

IX.

UNFORTUNATELY the tax recommended to the states in November 1777 failed, and the sums derived from loans were greatly inadequate to the expenditures for the support of the war; and although the affairs of the states had experienced a favourable turn in 1778, the depreciation of the notes, under the unavoidable necessity of largely increased issues, grew rapidly greater. The emissions authorized during the year aggregated sixty-three million five hundred thousand dollars; the whole sum of bills emitted up to the 1st of January 1779 being one hundred and one million five hundred thousand. The solid cash passing through the continental treasury during the year was only seventy-eight thousand six hundred and sixty-six dollars, and in 1779 but seventy-three thousand dollars—so that the whole machinery of government was carried on for two entire years, so far as the agency of coin was concerned, with one hundred and fifty-one thousand six hundred and sixty-six dollars! So small an expenditure of metallic currency shows the powerful agency of paper in the war operations of that critical period, performing as it did, in spite of counterfeits and depreciation, the office of hard money.[1]

---

[1] BRECK.—"This handful of coin in gold would weigh but seven hundred pounds; and we may not be surprised at the government being so chary as to refuse General WASHINGTON'S demand for a small share

2. According to THOMAS JEFFERSON'S table the cash value of the emissions authorized in 1778 was somewhat more than eleven million three hundred and thirty thousand dollars. The depreciation in January and February was four paper dollars for one in silver; in March five for one; in April six for one; in May five for one; in June and July four for one; in August and September five for one; in November and December six for one.[1] The rise in value in June and July was due to intelligence of the French alliance.

3. The year was but a repetition of the financial difficulties and embarrassments of 1777. "Let those among you who have leisure and opportunity," said Congress, in an address to the public in May, "collect the moneys which individuals in your neighbourhood are desirous of placing in the public funds. Let the several legislatures sink their respective issues, that so there being but one kind of bills there may be less danger of counterfeits. Refrain a little while from purchasing those things that are not absolutely necessary, so that they who have engrossed commodities may suffer (as they deservedly will) the loss of their ill-gotten hoards." Later, in the last days of December, it was considered important officially to deny reports "circulated in divers parts," that "Congress would not redeem the bills issued by them to defray the expenses of the war, but would suffer them to sink

of it to pay bounties to enlisted soldiers. In denying him Congress declared that the coin must be kept for the commissaries of prisoners, to be used where paper would not pass."

[1] It is to be observed that the depreciation was greater in some states than in others at the same moment.

in the hands of the holders." Such allegations were denounced as false and derogatory to their honour. And doubtless at that time the confident belief was that the bills would be paid to the uttermost.

X.

NOTWITHSTANDING, however, the great helps received from France of men, ships and money, and the widespread hopes which the alliance with that great empire had excited, the financial circumstances of both Congress and the states were daily growing more embarrassing and gloomy. With a view to radical improvement in the public credit, Congress signalized the opening of the year 1779 with measures of substantial importance. On the 2d of January—besides calling out of circulation the bills authorized the 20th of May 1777 and the 11th of April 1778,[1] both of which emissions had been so extensively counterfeited as practi-

[1] That great source of moral turpitude, the circulating paper, died of itself without any visible wound, except from the immense quantity counterfeited in New York and elsewhere under British influence. In a confidential letter to Lord GEORGE GERMAINE, about this time (1781), General CLINTON observed, "that the experiments suggested by your lordships have been tried; no assistance that could be drawn from the power of gold *or the arts of counterfeiting* have been left untried, but still the currency, like the widow's cruise of oil, has not failed."—[GORDON's *History of the American Revolution.*] "It is a fact too well authenticated to admit of dispute," says HENRY PHILLIPS, Jr., "that General HOWE aided the making and altering of counterfeit continental bills. In the same newspaper—in New York—in which the British official documents were printed, were also printed advertisements proposing to supply counterfeit money to persons going into other colonies; so nearly and exactly executed that no risk attended their circulation. Persons accompanying a British flag of truce were known to have made use of the opportunity for circulating the counterfeits; and emissaries from New York endeavoured to obtain from the mills paper similar to that used by Congress for its emissions."—[PHILLIPS's *Continental Money*, ii. 70.]

cally to destroy their value—Congress appealed to the states to pay into the continental treasury their respective quotas of fifteen millions of dollars for the year 1779, and six millions a year for eighteen years from and after 1779; the whole sums so paid to be a fund for sinking the loans and emissions made prior to the 31st of December following. So much of it as was derived from the yearly payments of six millions was to be devoted in the first instance to the payment of interest on loans made and to be made up to the 1st of January 1780, and secondly, to the redemption of the principal of loans contracted up to the same date. The residue, together with the amount derived from the fifteen millions to be paid during the year 1779, was not to be reissued but destroyed. And finally, the bills issued by Congress prior to 1780 were alone to be received on account of the quotas. Three days later taxes to the amount of fifteen millions were allotted among the states; Georgia was exempted from the apportionment, that state being occupied by British troops.—On the 21st of May, in consequence of the extreme depreciation of the paper, in addition to the fifteen millions asked for in January, the states were called upon to supply, for the service of the year 1779, their several quotas of forty-five millions—the whole to be paid into the continental treasury before the 1st of January 1780. On the 6th of October, Congress, accommodating itself to the depreciation as it then stood, and still hoping that the taxes already called for—if duly collected—would stop it where it was, and answer the demands on the public till February following, called on the states to pay into the treasury on the first of that month, and on the first day of each succeeding month to the 1st of October 1780, inclusive, their respective quotas of the further sum of fifteen millions of dollars.

Each of these calls was accompanied by circular letters addressed to the states. "Suddenly called upon," said the first of these, "to repel the unprovoked invasion of a prince who ought to have exerted himself for our protection; without arms or ammunition, without military discipline or permanent finances, without an established government and without allies, and enfeebled by habitual attachments to our very enemies, we were precipitated into all the expensive operations relative to a state of war with one of the most formidable nations on earth. Surrounded on all sides with wants, difficulties and dangers, notwithstanding the internal wealth of our country, immediate taxation was impracticable. And for the same reason, and a share of ill success at different periods, we could not hope, either at home or abroad, to borrow money to supply our exigencies. From necessity we embraced the expedient of emitting paper money on the faith of the United States; an expedient often successfully practised in separate states while we were subjected to British dominion. Large sums were indispensably necessary, and the paper currency multiplied beyond what was necessary for the purposes of a circulating medium. This alone could not fail to discredit it in some degree, but the arts of an unprincipled enemy have added to the mischief. As their last effort, they have had recourse to fraud. Their emissaries have employed a variety of artifices to debase our money and increase the prices of commodities. The fears and apprehensions of the people have been alarmed by misrepresentations, while our enemies of the highest rank have not hesitated to counterfeit our bills of credit and disperse them through the country. Such being the embarrassments which interrupt the free circulation of our money, they loudly call for a remedy, and Congress, from a regard for good faith, for private justice and the public safety, are bound to apply it. To raise the value of our paper money and to redeem it will not, we are persuaded, be difficult. Without public inconvenience or private distress, the whole of the debt incurred in paper emissions to this day may be cancelled by taxes; it may be cancelled within a period so limited as must leave the possessor of the bills satisfied with his security, and if, by a continuance of the war, the public service should demand further emissions, they, too, may be cancelled within the same period; it being evident that our ability to sustain a tax must increase in proportion to the quantity of money in circulation." "The great and increasing depreciation of your currency," said the second of these addresses, issued in May, "requires the immediate, strenuous and united efforts of all true friends of the country. In vain will it be for your delegates to form plans of economy, to strive to stop continued emissions by loans or taxation, if you do not zealously co-operate with them in promoting their designs, and use your utmost industry to prevent waste of money in expenditure, which your respective situations in the places where it is expended may enable you to do. A discharge of this duty and a compliance with recommendations for supplying money, may enable Congress to give speedy assurances that no more emissions shall take place, and thereby end that source of depreciation. We are persuaded you will take all possible care that the public welfare interfere as little as may be with the comfort and ease of individuals; and though raising these sums will press heavily on some of your constituents, yet the obligations we feel for your venerable clergy, the truly helpless widows and orphans, your most gallant, generous and meritorious officers and soldiers, and the public faith and common weal, so irresistibly urge us to attempt the appreciation of your currency that we cannot withhold obedience to those authoritative sensations. To our constituents we submit the propriety and purity of our intentions, well knowing they will not forget that we lay no burden upon them but those in which we participate with them; a happy sympathy that pervades society formed on the basis of equal liberty. Many cares, many labours—and may we not add reproaches? —are peculiar to us. These are the emoluments of our unsolicited stations, and with these we are content if you approve our conduct." In the brief letter of the 9th of October Congress said: "The money which Congress is at liberty to emit (the limit of emissions had been fixed on the 1st of September preceding at $200,000,000, of which a considerable amount was as yet unauthorized), will probably be expended in the beginning of December next, and subsequent supplies must be furnished by the states. This evinces the necessity of punctual payment of the respective quotas, on which their public credit, the existence of their arms and the support of their liberties so greatly depend. We are deeply concerned to find the sums required are so large, but since the emissions are limited we doubt not that the operations of the taxes and other salutary measures in the course of the year will reduce prices, and enable Congress to lessen the quotas, or apply a part of them to diminish the public debt. To promote so desirable an object we, on our part, will endeavour to observe the strictest economy in the public expenditures."

Unhappily the states did not respond to these appeals in any adequate degree.

2. "A compliance with these requisitions," said a committee of Congress in April 1781, "would not only have answered the exigencies of the year (that is, the year 1789), but would have arrested depreciation in its progress. But as they were not complied with in due time, and the demands of the public were pressing and constant, the prospect of future taxes served only to urge those who had in their possession the supplies and accessaries wanted to enhance the price in order to pay their taxes with greater ease, while the treasury, receiving no recruit from taxes, was from time to time replenished with new emissions —and from these causes combined, the depreciation, instead of receiving a check, proceeded with redoubled vigour."

The emissions authorized between the 1st of January and the 1st of September 1779 aggregated one hundred millions of dollars, and from the 1st of September to the 29th of November, when the last emission was authorized, the aggregate sum of emissions was forty millions—making a total for the year of one hundred and forty millions; and from the first emission in June 1775 to September 1st 1779 of one hundred and sixty millions ($159,948,880); the coin value of the emissions of 1779 ($140,052,280) being, according to THOMAS JEFFERSON'S table, seven millions three hundred and twenty-nine thousand two hundred and seventy-eight dollars. The depreciation, according to the same authority, was—January 14th, eight for one; February 3d and 12th, ten for one; April 2d, seventeen for one; May 5th, twenty-four for one; June 4th and 17th, twenty for one; September 17th, twenty-four for one; October 14th, thirty for one; November 17th and 29th, thirty-eight and a half for one.

3. As there was a general outcry because of the depreciation and the floods of money in circulation, Congress resolved on the 1st of September that they would on no account whatever emit more bills than enough to make the whole amount up to two hundred millions. Forty million fifty-one thousand one hundred and twenty dollars being the sum necessary to conclude the two hundred millions, it was determined that only so much thereof be emitted as should be absolutely necessary for the public exigencies before adequate supplies could be otherwise obtained, relying for such supplies on the exertions of the states.[1]

4. On the 13th of September Congress issued an elaborate address, exhaustive of the condition of the financial affairs of the country. Money, said the authors of this important paper, was necessary to

[1] Report of Committee of Congress, 18th April 1781.

create, pay and supply the army. "Of your own, there was at the beginning of the war but little; of no nation in the world could you then borrow." Bills of credit were emitted of necessity, and the faith of the people was pledged for their payment, and loans were solicited and obtained. A national debt was unavoidably created. The sum of the debt on which interest was payable in France was $7,545,196; on which interest was payable in America $26,188,909; the amount borrowed abroad was not exactly known, the balances not having been transmitted, but was supposed to be about $4,000,000. The aggregate taxes paid into the continental treasury were stated at $3,027,560; so that all the funds advanced by the people in the form of loans and taxes were but $36,761,665. "Judge then of the necessity of emissions, and learn from whom and whence that necessity arose." "We unanimously declare it essential to the welfare of the states that the taxes already called for be immediately paid into the treasury." "Exclusive of the great expenses of the war, the depreciation of the currency has swelled the price of every necessary article, and of consequence has made such additions to the usual amount of expenditure that very considerable supplies must be immediately provided by taxes and loans." The physical ability of the States to pay its debts was elaborately argued, while the excellence of the circulation provided by Congress was alleged in a well-known phrase: "Let it be remembered that paper money is the only kind of money which cannot 'make wings unto itself and fly away.' It remains with us; it will not forsake us; it is ever ready and at hand for the purposes of commerce or taxes, and every industrious man can find it." It had been charged by the enemies of America that there was reason to apprehend a violation of the public faith. This imputation was indignantly repelled. "It is with great regret and reluctance," said the authors of the paper from which we are quoting, "that we can prevail on ourselves to take the least notice of a question which involves in it a doubt so injurious to the honour and dignity of America." "We should pay an ill compliment to the understanding and honour of every true American were we to adduce many arguments to show the baseness or bad policy of violating our national faith, or omitting to pursue the measures necessary to preserve it. A bankrupt faithless republic would be a novelty in the political world, and appear among reputable nations like a common prostitute among chaste and respectable matrons. The pride of America revolts from the idea: her citizens know for what purposes these emissions were made, and have repeatedly plighted their faith for the redemption of them; they are to be found in every man's possession, and every man is interested in their being redeemed: they must therefore entertain a high opinion of American credulity, who suppose the people capable of believing, on due reflection, that all America will, against the faith, the honour and the interest of all America, be ever prevailed upon to countenance, support or permit, so ruinous, so disgraceful a measure. . . . . Determine to finish the contest as you began it, honestly and gloriously. Let it never be said that America had no sooner become independent, than she became insolvent; or that her infant glories and growing fame were obscured and tarnished by broken contracts and violated faith, in the very hour when all the nations of the earth were admiring, and almost adoring, the splendour of her rising."

XI.

THE campaign of the year had been barren of important results. On the part of the British it had been predatory; one of robbery, burning and destruction; on the part of the Americans defensive, although the actions at Stony Point and Powles Hook were notable instances of their enterprise and valour. Georgia, however, was substantially recovered to the Crown; and the British, seeing in the condition and circumstances of the Southern States opportunity for successful operations, made vigorous preparations for a winter and spring campaign in that portion of the country. The means of defence were inconsiderable; and Congress, deeply impressed with the importance of impending events—not only in the South but in the North also—exerted all its powers to provide for the crisis. The condition of the treasury was one of anxious solicitude. Empty, and greatly in arrears, taxes and loans utterly inadequate, prevented from further emissions of paper money by a solemn pledge to the people,[1] the army unpaid, the subsistence de-

[1] "The situation of the army with respect to supplies is beyond description alarming. It has been five or six weeks past on half allowance, and we have not more than three days' bread at a third allowance on hand, nor anywhere within reach. When this is exhausted we must depend on the precarious gleanings of the neighbouring country. Our magazines are absolutely empty everywhere, and our commissaries entirely destitute of money or credit to replenish them. We have never

partment unsupplied,—a new mode of requisition was now adopted by the Congress. On the 25th of February the states were called upon to furnish, for the campaign of 1780, supplies in kind, to be raised and delivered at such times and places as the commander-in-chief of the army should fix upon as most convenient. The call was for 330,000 hundred weight of beef; 455,000 gallons of rum; 123,000 barrels of flour; 695,000 bushels of corn or other short forage equivalent; 53,000 bushels of salt; 9000 tons of hay; 7000 hogsheads of tobacco, and 52,000 bushels of rice. The accounts of the states for these supplies were to be kept and settled in Spanish milled dollars, and the balances ultimately paid in specie; and if, upon final adjustment, any state was found to have supplied more than its quota under the call, the value of the surplus was to be paid for in specie, and interest allowed at the rate of six per cent. a year; while, if any state failed in delivering its quota, it was to be charged with the aggregate sum of the deficiency, and pay to the United States a like interest thereon. None of the states complied with this call, nor did anything approximating to a compliance. Later in the year, on

---

experienced a like extremity at any period of the war. We have often felt temporary want from accidental delays in forwarding supplies, but we always had something in our magazines and the means of procuring more. Neither one nor the other is at present the case. This representation is the result of a minute examination of our resources."—[WASHINGTON to President REED, December 16th 1779.] "Our provisions are in a manner gone. We have not a ton of hay at command, nor magazines to draw from. * * Money is extremely scarce, and worth little when we get it. We have been so poor for a fortnight that we could not forward the public despatches for want of cash to support the expresses."—[General GREENE to President REED, February 29th 1780.]

the 4th of November, a similar requisition was made for taxes amounting to ten millions of dollars in gold or silver, or "money of the new emission,"—or specific articles enumerated in the call and to be supplied at fixed prices, and upon terms the same as those which accompanied the call of the 25th of February. In the interim between these two dates, several appeals were made to particular states; September 15th notably, when Massachusetts, New Hampshire and Connecticut were asked, for the "immediate supply of the army," to furnish one thousand head of cattle weekly; and New Jersey, Pennsylvania and Delaware were urged "with all possible despatch" to supply two thousand head for instant wants. It illustrates the extreme poverty of Congress during this important year, that it was compelled to draw warrants to the amount of $28,300, on the loan-offices, for means necessary to defray the expenses of forwarding the cattle to the army.

XII.

THE depreciation of the bills was now (March 18th 1780) so excessive, and the disorders it occasioned so wide-spread and important, that Congress resolved upon a vital modification of their character. "These United States having been driven into this just and necessary war at a time when no regular civil governments were established of sufficient energy to enforce the collection of taxes, or to furnish funds for the redemption of such bills of credit as their necessities obliged them to issue, and before the powers of Europe were sufficiently convinced of the justice of their cause, or of the probable event of the controversy, to afford them aid or credit; in consequence of which their bills increased in quantity beyond the sum necessary for the purposes of a circulating medium,—and wanting at the same time specific funds upon which to rest for their redemption, they have seen them daily sink in value, notwithstanding every effort that has been made to support them; insomuch that they are now passed, by common consent in most parts of the United States, at at least thirty-nine fortieths below their nominal value, and still depreciating,—whereby the community suffers great injustice, the public finances are deranged, and the necessary dispositions for the defence of the country are impeded and perplexed; to remedy these evils, for which purpose the United States are now become competent,—their independence being well assured, their civil governments established and vigorous, and the spirit of their citizens ardent for exertion,—it is essential speedily to reduce the quantity of the paper medium in circulation, and to establish and appropriate funds that shall insure the punctual redemption of the bills," Congress resolved, that the respective states should continue to bring into the continental treasury, by taxes or otherwise, their full quotas of the fifteen millions of dollars assigned among them on the 6th of October 1779; that silver and gold should be received in payment of the taxes at the rate of one Spanish milled dollar in lieu of forty dollars of the bills; that the bills so brought in (except those for January and February, which were required to discharge past contracts), should not be reissued but destroyed; that as rapidly as such bills were brought in and funds should be provided, other bills should be issued, not to exceed on any account a twentieth part of the nominal sum of the bills brought in to be destroyed; that the new bills to be issued should be redeemable in specie after six years, with interest at five per cent., also to be paid in specie at the time of redemption, or at the election of the holder annually in sterling bills of exchange drawn upon the American commissioners in Europe at 4*s.* 6*d.* sterling per dollar. The new bills were to be issued on the funds of the individual states, to be established by them for the purpose of redemption, and the faith of the United States was also pledged as an additional security, in case any state should be rendered incapable to redeem them. The new bills were to be issued by the continental treasury, and six-tenths of them were to be delivered to the states in their proper proportions; four-tenths to be for the use of the United States, and credited to the states in adjustment of their quotas under the call of 6th of October 1779; the states to be charged with whatever portion of the interest was paid by the United States in bills of exchange; and finally, they were called on to provide funds for their several quotas of the new bills, to be so productive as to sink or redeem one-sixth part of them annually after the first of the ensuing January (1781).

It is not worth while to dwell upon this act; it was denounced by Doctor WITHERSPOON as a "great and deliberate breach of the public faith;" the Count de VERGENNES said it was "an act of bankruptcy," and other public men were equally bitter in their expressions concerning it. The reader can judge for himself—in view of all the circumstances—how far the Congress was censurable, or whether it was so at all or not.

The statesmen of Congress offered this scheme to the states in the confident hope and belief that it would be accepted with punctuality; that it would restore the currency to a fixed standard; that it would enable the states to furnish the supplies called for on the 25th of February; and that it would put Congress in a position to pay the army, discharge the more pressing debts already contracted, and provide means for the exigencies of the campaign. But the states did not respond, as Congress so strongly hoped; and public necessities again compelled the adoption of temporary expedients. Among these was that of raising funds by drawing bills of exchange on the American ministers in Europe; although, as was afterwards with extreme simplicity admitted, Congress had not sufficient assurance that the bills would be honoured. The whole amount of these foreign bills authorized to be drawn, including those intended to pay interest on the public debt, approximated to near three-quarters of a million of dollars.

On the 20th of March the states were recommended to so modify their tender laws as to conform them to the existing state of the currency, and to take care so to frame them as to prevent unjust advantage being taken of the proposed action of the legislatures. The states complied, though it is hardly necessary to remark that it was impossible to prevent fraud and injustice, however vigilant the assemblies were to attempt it.

XIII.

On the 24th of April Congress made another appeal to the states: "It is the duty of Congress to be as full and explicit in their requisitions as the public exigencies are great and pressing; and they are confident that the citizens of the states are not more desirous to be informed of their affairs than they are ready to afford the most vigorous assistance. It is unnecessary to mention our embarrassments; they are known to you; to the means of relieving them we wish to call your attention. The whole of the moneys due on the quotas of taxes to the 1st of March last are become of immediate and indispensable necessity. On these quotas drafts are now making and must continue to be made to the whole amount, nor can a doubt be admitted of their being punctually answered. If any state be unprepared, if the collections are incomplete, not a moment is to be lost. Delay may involve consequences too fatal to be hazarded. Urge, therefore, the instant execution of every measure which has been adopted, and the speedy adoption of such as yet remain to be taken. The crisis calls for exertion. Much is to be done in a little time, and every motive that can stimulate the mind of man presents itself to view. No period has occurred in this long and glorious struggle in which indecision could be so destructive; and on the other hand no conjuncture has been more favourable to great and deciding efforts."

2. On the 19th of May Congress called upon the states from New Hampshire to Virginia—those two states included—to collect and pay into the public treasury, within thirty days, ten millions of dollars in continental currency, part of the sum required to be paid last year. The states, in order to comply, pressed the collection of the taxes, which occasioned so much clamour on the part of those who had furnished supplies on credit, that on the 27th of May the legislatures were recommended to empower the collectors of continental taxes due before the 1st of March 1780, to receive in payment of them the notes or certificates which had been given by the quartermaster and commissary of purchases for supplies.

XIV.

DURING this year [1780] Congress directed its efforts to the reforming of abuses, and a more responsible administration of the army funds and supplies. In every department there had been peculation and wastefulness. There was a good deal of complaint at a very early period touching these things, to which no special heed had been given; at any rate not in any effective official way; but at length, in May 1779, the matter came before Congress. The Board of Treasury, on the 28th of that month, reported that in the judgment of its members it would be impracticable to carry on the war with paper money at the existing enormous expenditures made by the departments of the commissary and quartermaster generals, and of the medical director. The Board said that an opinion generally prevailed among the people that one cause of the alarming cost of those departments arose from allowing commissions to the numerous persons employed in purchasing for the army, and that there was a wide dissatisfaction in consequence. A committee was appointed to inquire into and report upon the subject. On the 9th of July the committee reported, recommending to the executive powers of the states instantly to make strict inquiry into the conduct of every person within their several jurisdictions employed in any of the departments charged, and to suspend and cause the prosecution of those guilty or strongly suspected. Later, in August 1780, Congress declared that it was of the utmost importance to prevent waste, destruction, embezzlement and misapplication of the public stores; and as no adequate means had been provided for the just punishment of delinquents in the various military departments, it was resolved [it is to be observed that the *resolves* of Congress were substantially *acts* of Congress, intended to have the effect and force of laws so far as they went] that any one who should sell, embezzle or wilfully misapply the military or hospital stores, horses, arms or ammunition, *should suffer death*, or such other punishment as a court-martial should deem equal to the punishment of the offender.

2. "In addition to short crops (speaking of the years 1779 and 1780) and depreciating money, disorder and confusion pervaded the departments for supplying the army. Systems for these purposes had been hastily adopted, and were very inadequate to the ends proposed. To provide for an army under the best establishment and with a full military chest is a work of difficulty, and, though guarded by the precautions which time and experience have suggested, opens a door to many frauds; but it was the hard case of the Americans to be called on to discharge this duty without knowledge of the business, and under ill-digested systems and with a paper currency never two days of the same value. Abuses crept in, frauds were practised, economy was exiled. To obviate these evils Congress adopted the expedient of sending a committee to the camp of the main army. They were fur-

nished with ample powers and instructions to reform abuses, to alter preceding systems and to establish new ones in their room. The committee proceeded to camp in May 1780, and thence wrote sundry letters to Congress and the states, in which they confirmed the representations made of the distresses and disorders everywhere prevalent.[1] In particular they stated—that the army was unpaid for five months; that it seldom had more than six days' provisions in advance, and was on several occasions for successive days without meat; that the army was destitute of forage; that the medical department had neither sugar, coffee, tea, chocolate, wine nor spirituous liquors of any kind; that every department of the army was without money, and had not even the shadow of credit left; that the patience of the soldiers, borne down by the pressure of complicated sufferings, was on the point of being exhausted."[2]

---

[1] President Reed, in his message to the Assembly of Pennsylvania in 1779, says: "In conformity to the laws of the state and your desire, we have proceeded to the sale of the confiscated estates, and have the satisfaction to acquaint you that the sums arising therefrom are so considerable as to afford a great relief to the good people of this state from their public burdens."

[2] Ramsay, ii. 189.

XV.

Now, here are some facts concerning the constitution of the army: The first enlistments into the continental service expired at the end of the year 1775. The commander-in-chief, not being able to re-enlist the soldiers, was reduced almost to the necessity of abandoning the extensive lines in the vicinity of Boston; but notwithstanding this, such were the prejudices in favour of short enlistments, and such the dread of a standing army, that Congress was obliged to enlist the second army for one year, and the time of its service expired at or about the end of 1776. During that campaign Congress was so fully convinced of the fatal consequences of such a policy as at all events to determine that the next enlistments should be for the war; but was afterwards constrained to provide the alternative, "or for three years,"—and those who enlisted for this term left the army in 1780. In 1780 the army was greatly reduced, and the states were earnestly called on to recruit their respective regiments,—but such were the prospects of gain from privateering and other employments—such had been the sufferings of the army, and so weakened was the confidence in public faith, as to require enormous bounties in specie for obtaining recruits; the average bounty in many states was two hundred and fifty dollars in specie, and in Massachusetts it was upwards of two hundred and eighty. If we divide the army into four classes it will appear that the soldiers of the first and second classes were discharged and fully paid in 1775 and 1776; that the soldiers of the third class, who enlisted for the war between 1777 and 1780, served six, five or four years, without any other prospect of reward than the stipulations of Congress; and that the fourth class, some of whom served two and a half years, others two years and others one, were amply paid by bounties, the least of which amounted to one hundred dollars a year, or eight and one-third dollars a month in specie, exclusive of the allowance made by Congress. The third and fourth classes were, however, entitled by their contract to six and two-third dollars in specie per month, or to an equivalent exclusive of bounties, rations and clothing.[1]

2. Until the opening of the campaign of 1780 the army had borne its sufferings with unparalleled patience and perseverance. What pay they had received was chiefly depreciated money. But Congress was not unmindful of their sufferings and services. As early as September 1776 it was resolved to make provision for granting lands in certain proportions to the officers and soldiers who would engage in the service and continue therein to the close of the war or until discharged by Congress, and to the representatives of such officers and soldiers as might be slain by the enemy. On the 15th of May 1778 it was unanimously resolved that all military officers commissioned by Congress, who were then or who thereafter might be in the service

---

[1] ELBRIDGE GERRY in House of Representatives, 18th February 1790: "Debates in Congress," ii. 1325–6.

of the United States and continue therein during the war, should, after the conclusion thereof, receive annually for the term of seven years, if they lived so long, one-half of the pay then established for such officers, with a proviso that general officers should not receive more than the half-pay of a colonel; and it was resolved also that non-commissioned officers and soldiers enlisted for the war should receive at the expiration of it, a reward of eighty dollars. On the 17th of August 1779, having prefaced their resolution with a preamble setting forth that the army of the United States of America, by their patriotism, valour and perseverance in the defence of the rights and liberties of the country, were entitled to the gratitude as well as approbation of their fellow-citizens, they recommended to the several states to make such further provision for the officers and soldiers enlisted for the war as belonged to them respectively, and who should continue in service till the establishment of peace, as should be an adequate compensation for the many dangers, losses and hardships they had suffered in the course of the contest; either by granting to their officers half-pay for life and proper rewards to their soldiers, or in such other way as might appear most expedient. And it was recommended also that the states should make provision for the widows of such of their officers and soldiers who had enlisted for the war, as had died or might die in the service, as would secure to them the sweets of that liberty for the attainment of which their husbands had laid down their lives. On the 10th of April 1780, Congress resolved that so soon as the state of the public finances would admit, they would make good to the line of the army and the independent corps, the deficiency of their original pay occasioned by the depreciation of the currency; but none were to derive the benefit of this resolution except those who had engaged to serve for the war or for three years, and were then in service, or should thereafter engage to serve during the war. On the 13th of August 1780, Congress resolved that from and after the first of that month the army should receive their pay in the "new bills," and again recommended to such of the states as had not made compensation to their officers and soldiers, agreeably to the resolution of Congress of the 17th August 1779, to do so as soon as possible. At the same time the provision for granting lands was extended to the general officers; and on the 24th the resolution of May 1778, granting half-pay for seven years to officers who should continue in service to the end of the war, was extended to the generals and such as had died or should thereafter die in the service, to commence from the time of such officers' death; or if there should be no widow, or in case of her intermarriage, that it should go to the orphan children of such marriage. But still the public treasury remained unsupplied; the army continued without pay, and oftentimes were in great distress for want of provisions.[1]

[1] Report of Committee of Congress, 18th May 1781.

XVI.

The distress which the Americans suffered from the diminished value of their currency, though felt in the year 1778, did not arrive at its highest pitch till the year 1780. Under the pressure of sufferings from this cause, the officers of the Jersey line addressed a memorial to their state legislature, setting forth, "that four months' pay of a private would not procure for his family a single bushel of wheat; that the pay of a colonel would not purchase oats for his horse; that a common labourer or expressman received four times as much pay as an American officer." They urged that unless a speedy and ample remedy was provided a dissolution of their line was inevitable, and concluded by saying that their pay should be made up in Mexican dollars or in something equivalent.[1]

2. The original idea of a continental army, to be raised, paid, subsisted and regulated upon an equal and uniform principle, had been in a great measure exchanged for state establishments. This mischievous measure partly originated from necessity, for state credit was not quite so much depreciated as continental; Congress not possessing the means for supporting the army, devolved the business on the component parts of the confederacy. Some states, from their internal ability and advantages, furnished their troops

---

[1] Ramsay, ii. 184.

not only with clothing but with many conveniences. Others supplied theirs with some necessaries, but on a more contracted scale. A few, from their particular situation, could do little or nothing at all.[1]

3. So great were the necessities of the American army, that WASHINGTON was obliged to call on the magistrates of the adjacent counties for specific quantities of provisions, to be supplied in a given number of days. At other times he was compelled to send out detachments of his troops to take provisions at the point of the bayonet.[2]

4. But though a tide of misfortunes appeared to be pouring in upon the United States, no signs were discovered of any disposition to relinquish the struggle. "They seemed to rise in the midst of their distresses, and to gain strength from the pressure of calamities." When Congress could command neither money nor credit, the citizens of Philadelphia formed a bank—called the "Bank of Pennsylvania"—the sole object of which was to furnish the army with a large supply of rations. This institution was the project of ROBERT MORRIS, who, in conjunction with others, his fellow-citizens, subscribed altogether 315,000*l.* Pennsylvania money. The subscribers to the bank pledged themselves to pay their subscriptions in gold and silver, if it became necessary in order to fulfil its engagements, while Congress, to indemnify and reimburse them, directed the Board of Treasury to deposit in the bank 150,000*l.* sterling bills of exchange. The usefulness of this institution was great, and it was all the greater because the times were out of joint and

---

[1] RAMSAY, ii. 185. [2] RAMSAY, ii. 186.

critical. The "Bank of Pennsylvania" continued its operations for about a year, and was the ground-work of the "Bank of America," established in 1781.

5. The powers of the committee of Congress in the camp of the General-in-Chief were so enlarged as to authorize them to frame and execute plans for drawing out the resources of the country. In this character they urged the states to prompt and vigorous exertions; but though the legislatures enacted laws and undertook their execution, they were only measurably successful. Touching this want of success in meeting the public exigencies, RAMSAY philosophizes thus: "The result of the experiment was, that however favourable republics may be to the liberty and happiness of the people in time of peace, they will be greatly deficient in that vigour and despatch which military operations require, unless they imitate the policy of monarchies by committing the executive department to a single will." Which is excellent good politics, but extremely unrepublican.

6. Family gifts—the gifts of affection to soldiers in the army—entered not inconsiderably into the sum total of its support, while the exertions of associated neighbours were also most useful. The ladies of Philadelphia—as an example of this—contributed of their means; the widow gave her mite, and the rich,—well, the rich did not give in the proportion of PHILLIS the coloured woman who gave 7*s.* 6*d.*, but they did extremely well, and on the 4th of July 1780, the wife of President REED wrote to WASHINGTON that the amount of their subscriptions was somewhat over three hundred thousand dollars ($300,634), and that

his orders were awaited as to the best plan of disposing of the money. The Marchioness DE LAFAYETTE gave one hundred guineas in specie to this fund, and the Countess DE LUZERNE—another French lady of rank—gave six thousand continental dollars, equivalent to $150 in cash.[1]

7. Notwithstanding all that was done, however, the army continued in distress and Congress in its embarrassments. On the 26th of August 1780, the states were earnestly recommended to take the most speedy and effectual measures for drawing in their respective quotas of the continental bills by taxes or otherwise, in order that the new money might be issued. And at the same time the states were further recommended to raise by taxes, payable in the new bills, their respective quotas of three millions of dollars, and to pay the same into the public treasury as speedily as possible, the whole payment to be completed by the last day of December following. From this it was hoped that Congress would draw a supply of money to enable them to pay the army and carry on the war with vigour; to discharge the unfunded debt, and pay the interest due on loan-office certificates. The consequences that ensued from the failure of the states to comply with this call, though alarming and painful to recollect, were far short of what might have been apprehended.[2]

---

[1] Life of President JOSEPH REED, 26, *et seq.*

[2] Report of Committee of Congress, April 18th 1781.

XVII.

Now the consequences, so alarming and painful to the public recollection, are summed up in a word—*mutiny.*

From a complication of wants and sufferings, a disposition to revolt began to show itself in the army. It broke forth into full action among the soldiers stationed at Fort Schuyler. Thirty-one men of that garrison went off in a body; being pursued, sixteen of them were overtaken, and thirteen of the sixteen were instantly killed. About the same time two regiments of Connecticut troops mutinied and got under arms. They determined to return home or gain subsistence at the point of the bayonet. Their officers reasoned with them, and urged every argument that could interest either their pride or their passions. They were reminded of their good conduct and of the important objects for which they were contending,—their answer was, "Our sufferings are too great, and we want present relief." After much expostulation, they were at length prevailed upon to return to duty. It is remarkable that this mutinous disposition of the Connecticut troops was in a great measure quelled by the Pennsylvania line, which in the course of a few months planned and executed a much more serious revolt than that which they now suppressed. On the night of the 1st of January 1781, a mutiny broke out among these. The whole line, except three regiments, mustered under arms and declared for a redress of grievances. They alleged that they had enlisted for three years or during the war; the three years were expired, and the men insisted that the choice of staying or going was in themselves. The officers contended that the choice was in the state. Superadded to this cause of dispute, were the real sufferings of the soldiers,—want of food, want of clothing, want of pay. The British tried to corrupt the mutineers; but the mutineers were not traitors; they arrested the British spies; delivered them into the hands of General WAYNE, and they were tried, condemned and executed. The difficulties which lay at the bottom of this revolt were finally adjusted; but the example was contagious. Some Jersey troops later in the month mutinied also; they were less wise than the Pennsylvanians; they proceeded to acts of outrage against particular officers, and professed obedience to others. The measures for reducing them to submission were prompt and energetic; two were executed, and the others were pardoned upon promise of future good behaviour.[1]

---

[1] See RAMSAY ii. 185, 219, *et seq.*

XVIII.

THE depreciation of the bills proceeded during the year very steadily down to the point of seventy-five continental dollars for one in cash. In January the exchange stood at forty for one; February, forty-seven for one; March and April, sixty for one; May, fifty-nine for one; June, sixty for one; July, sixty-four for one; August, seventy for one; September and October, seventy-two for one; November, seventy-four, and in December, seventy-five for one. A familiar instance of the effects of the depreciation was thus given by a writer in *The Pennsylvania Packet:* "I had money enough to buy a hogshead of sugar. I sold it again, and got a good deal more money than it cost me; yet what I sold it for, when I went to market again, would buy but a tierce. I sold that too for a great deal of profit, yet the whole of what I sold it for would afterwards buy but a barrel. I have now more money than I ever had, and yet I am not so rich as when I had less. I am sure we shall grow poorer and poorer unless we fall on some method to lower prices, and then the money we have to spare will be worth something."

2. The depreciation of 1780 was partly due to the want of decisive results in the war operations, and partly to continued emissions by the states. As an extreme example of this latter, Virginia authorized

emissions to an aggregate of thirty millions during the year, and made it a legal tender at forty for one! Other states did the same thing though less extensively; so that the steady increase in the volume of the currency steadily depressed its nominal value.

3. And it is a curious illustration of the laws which govern paper money, that as excessive issues had exiled the cash of the country from its accustomed place in the business of the people, it began to flow back as the paper money approached the period of its mortality. As this daily less capably performed the office of the instrument of exchange, gold and silver more certainly and amply flowed in to supply its place.

4. If all the taxes called for by Congress during the year had been paid into the treasury, they would have aggregated one hundred and eighty-six millions of dollars!

XIX.

THE exhausted state of the continental treasury and the universal disorder of the finances, the pressing demands for supplies in every department of the public service, the consequences which began to appear, and the confusion that threatened, became very serious and alarming at the beginning of the year 1781, and the public necessities had arisen to such a pitch of urgency as convinced all thinking men that a speedy remedy or ruin was in waiting.[1]

2. Though the revolts recited in a preceding paragraph had alarmed the states, they did not result in measures of permanent relief. The wants of the army were only partially supplied, and this chiefly by the exercise of military force, generally by seizing provisions and paying for them with a certificate which—as required by Congress—contained a statement on its face of the quantity and quality and price of what had been taken. But this sort of thing could not last; though in defiance of clamour Congress, impelled by the extremity of want, seriously thought of empowering the General-inChief to seize all the provisions he could find within twenty miles of his camp! During the whole winter and spring the army suffered untold privations,—without food, without clothing, often

[1] PELATIAH WEBSTER.

without fire even, they still clung—with a noble devotion—to the cause in which they were embarked.

3. On the 15th of January Congress, desirous of affording some immediate relief to these devoted men, made a requisition upon the states for eight hundred and seventy-nine thousand dollars ($879,342), to be paid in cash. "The arrears of pay due to the army," said Congress in an address accompanying this requisition, "demand your most serious consideration. The honour of government and military order and discipline depend on their regular discharge." But notwithstanding the smallness of the sum demanded, and the vital importance of the object to which it was to be devoted, Congress reported on the 18th of April that the requisition had not been answered!

4. About the beginning of the year JOHN LAURENS was sent to France, as a special minister, to seek further pecuniary aids from France. THE KING, notwithstanding the many demands upon his treasury for his own service, resolved to "give a new proof of his affection for the people of the United States," and granted a further subsidy of six millions of livres tournois; and also guaranteed the payment of a loan of ten millions made in Holland.[1] As the whole sum of the subsidy granted by THE KING would not probably be needed for demands in Europe, he consented that the remainder should be put at the disposal of the superintendent of finance for use in the United States.

5. Congress made a public statement (April 18th), showing the condition of the finances to the 10th of

[1] Mention has been made of this subsidy and guarantee in a former paragraph.

February. The foreign debt was computed at six millons, carrying a yearly interest of $360,000. The domestic debt (which included one hundred and sixty millions of old bills rated at seventy-five for one), was stated as being at a cash valuation $18,057,157, on seven millions of which ($7,313,306) interest was payable in bills of exchange on France, amounting to the yearly sum of $438,798.

XX.

It is at this point that we appropriately trace the history of the bills from the first of January to the time of their mortality in May. At the beginning of the year the idea that the bills were to depreciate to the point of no value whatever, and that such depreciation must be regarded as a tax upon the people [" depreciation," said Gouverneur Morris, in June 1780, " is an assessor that reaches every farthing and baffles every attempt to deceive"], began widely to prevail, and prepared the public mind for the catastrophe which soon befell them. The gradual character of the depreciation, latterly very much accelerated, however, had brought this particular phase of the currency question home to the understandings of most men; while the limited presence of real money, performing the business of exchange with celerity and perfect certainty, excited high hopes of a future stable and flourishing commerce.

On the 1st of January the exchange stood at seventy-five for one, and continued at that figure until about the 1st of March.

2. In order clearly to apprehend the circumstances which gave a final and fatal blow to the bills, and extinguished them utterly as the instrument of exchange, it is necessary that we retrace our steps backward into the spring of 1780. In March of that year the As-

sembly of Pennsylvania authorized an emission of 100,000*l.* paper bills, equivalent to about two hundred and sixty-six thousand dollars. In addition to carrying interest at five per cent., and the pledge of the faith of the state for their redemption, the assembly set apart as a further security a number of city lots in Philadelphia and the Province Island, at that time the property of the Commonwealth.—Hence the emission was called "the Island money." Although it was expected that, supported in this ample way, the bills would command their face-value, the fact was that they speedily depreciated. In order to remedy this, the assembly in December passed an act making them a legal tender, and added severe penalties for refusing to take them. This act, among other things, contained a clause which fixed the rate of the exchange between the continental and the province dollars at seventy-five for one; seventy-five of the former for one of the latter. This regulation was to continue until the 1st of February then next ensuing; after which date the State Executive Council was to publish the rate in the first week of each month; and as thus published it was to be the legal exchange between the continental and province money until the next publication. On the 2d of May 1781 one silver dollar was equal to three province dollars; and one province dollar was equal to seventy-five dollars of the continental bills; while at the same time the exchange between continental dollars and silver was 220 and 225 for one, to which point they had depreciated during March and April. The practice among the people was to multiply the published rate by three; so that when this was seventy-five for one, the exchange would be as between continental dollars and silver, 225 for one. When, therefore, on the 2d of May, the council fixed the rate between continental dollars and the island money at one hundred and seventy-five for one, they in effect fixed the exchange between continental dollars and silver at 525 for one. And this consequence immediately followed; and so vast and sudden a depreciation destroyed them utterly. They ceased to circulate as money, and were thenceforward objects only of curiosity and speculation. In this latter field, their value fluctuated from 500 to 1000 for one.[1]

3. THOMAS JEFFERSON says the public apprehension was, that the extinction of the bills would shake the confederacy to its very centre; but the result was entirely contrary to this gloomy anticipation; their annihilation was not only unattended by tumult, but was everywhere a matter of rejoicing and congratulation. Their great services as a support of the war were known and felt by all, and all knew and felt that their destruction was a certain public good.

4. But a single demonstration attended this great and important event. In Rhode Island—an obstreperous little commonwealth—some continental bills were buried with the honours of war. They were enclosed in a splendid repository, and over this a eulogy was pronounced as over the remains of a departed friend and benefactor. An emission of paper money had lately been made by the state; it was commonly called the "red money." During the ob-

[1] PELATIAH WEBSTER.

sequies of the continental bills, a pithy orator held up a bundle of the *red money,* with the expression, "Be thou also ready, for thou shalt surely die!" which soon happened.[1]

---

[1] SANDERSON: "Life of Robert Morris."

XXI.

CONGRESS, taught by a sad and disastrous experience the utter inefficiency of financial management by a "Board of Treasury," created a new officer. He was called the Superintendent of Finance. But, doubting the competency of any citizen of America to discharge the duties of so onerous and responsible a station, an appeal was made to an eminent foreigner, —who, pleading his advanced age, but declaring his interest in the cause of the American people, declined the office. This was Dr. PRICE.

2. ROBERT MORRIS was elected superintendent on the 21st of February 1781. He was a man of vast abilities and energy, and chose as his assistant GOUVERNEUR MORRIS,—a man not less able and determined than himself.

3. ROBERT MORRIS, perfectly apprehending the difficulties and dangers of this office, and resolute not to undertake it except upon conditions which would make him independent and absolute in its administration, dictated terms which excited great opposition. He insisted upon the power of appointing and discharging all persons who received or disbursed the public money. Congress protested and then yielded. The whole business of finance was comprised, he said, in two short and comprehensive sentences: in the first place, it was to collect the revenues in the way most

equal and easy to the people; in the second, to expend them frugally and honestly; and he required ample powers to effect these objects.

4. He found himself called upon — at the very threshold of office—to remedy great defects and substantially to reorganize the whole treasury service. Prodigality was a crying public evil; he retrenched with unflinching resolution. There was a multitude of unnecessary employees; he discharged them without fear or favour. In the places where confusion, wastefulness and weakness had reigned, he introduced order, economy and efficiency. He was not so fortunate, however, as—in stilted phrase—WEBSTER in later years described HAMILTON to have been. At the time of MORRIS'S appointment, the rock of the public credit—exhausted by repeated smitings—stubbornly refused to gush. But he drew from a fountain of greater honour and glory; it was that of a superb personal credit—and it did the business. The English were driven from the continent before he relinquished administration, and in a way which—though marked by many painful anxieties and sufferings—is yet highly satisfactory to read about; meaning, of course, as to final results.

5. WASHINGTON has described the condition of the army in the spring of 1781. "Instead of having magazines filled with provisions, we have a scanty pittance scattered here and there in the several states; instead of having arsenals well supplied with military stores, we are poorly provided, and the workmen all leaving them; instead of the various articles of field

equipage ready to deliver, the quartermaster-general is but now applying to the several states (as the dernier ressort) to provide these things for their troops respectively; instead of a regular system of transportation, established upon credit or funds in the quartermaster's hands to defray the contingent expenses of it, we have neither one nor the other; and all that business, or a great part of it, being done by military impressment, we are daily and hourly oppressing the people, souring their tempers and alienating their affections. In a word, instead of having everything in readiness to take the field, we have nothing, and instead of the prospect of a glorious offensive campaign, we have a bewildered and gloomy prospect of a defensive one."

6. It is quite impracticable to exhibit in detail the methods adopted by Mr. MORRIS to satisfy the clamours of creditors (he found the treasury two and a half millions in arrears at his entrance), and to supply the indispensable wants of the army. Among these, however, were considerable anticipations of funds provided in Europe for the service of the year 1782, and a prompt and extensive use of his own credit and that of his friends. As an example of this latter, in May—the treasury being utterly exhausted—he drew upon General PHILIP SCHUYLER, then in command at Albany, and Governor LOWREY, of New Jersey, for one thousand barrels of flour each, for which he pledged himself both as a public officer and a private man to pay in hard money within two months. Without immediate relief WASHINGTON would

have been driven to *put the laws of necessity in force,* which it was the object of Mr. MORRIS to avoid and prevent. "I shall make it a point to provide the money," he said, "being determined never to make an engagement that cannot be fulfilled; for if by any means I should fail in this respect, I shall quit my office as useless from that moment." He hurried forward as rapidly as it was possible to do, and in as great quantities as were possible to be obtained, the specific supplies that had been called for by Congress. The Eastern States provided as abundantly as they were able to do at the time, meat, salt and liquors. About this time—that is to say, during the summer of 1781—he undertook to furnish, during the current year, all the requisitions of Congress upon Pennsylvania, which consisted chiefly of flour, and were to be reimbursed out of the proceeds of taxes laid by a late act of the assembly upon the people of the state. Congress approved the contract as beneficial to the interests of the United States; it involved the sum of one million one hundred and twenty thousand dollars, and the supplies were furnished in anticipation before the money was obtained from the state treasury. As fiscal agent of Pennsylvania, he so managed the paper emissions of the state as to appreciate their value from six for one up to two for one. He had agents at all the important military stations; and though it was an absolute impossibility, political and financial, to supply the army as it ought to have been supplied, or even to furnish it adequately with essential things, he so contrived his management as to afford relief in the hours of extremity. Had he exhibited too great resources, the executive powers of the states would have relaxed their efforts; they did less than their share as it was, and MORRIS was censured that he did not do more; and he was constrained by the exigencies of his situation many times to deny succours that his great heart would willingly have supplied had his resources been equal to his wishes. "The late movements of the army," he wrote on the 20th of September 1781, "have so entirely drained me of money that I have been obliged to pledge my personal credit very deeply, besides borrowing from my friends and advancing, to promote the public service, every *shilling of my own.*" He issued his own promissory notes in large amounts —in the first year of his administration to a million and a half—and other notes—amounting in the aggregate to five hundred and eighty thousand dollars—signed by himself and payable at different times out of foreign funds and revenues of the United States, which circulated through the states and served the purposes of money. He went in person to the army of General WASHINGTON to inquire into its wants. He states in his diary (August 21st 1781) that while at head-quarters he had constant applications for money from almost everybody, as *all* had claims on the public treasury. But in a word, arms and ammunition, pay of troops and subsistence stores, were supplied upon the private resources of ROBERT MORRIS. He bore upon his broad and ample shoulders, to the close of the war, almost the whole pecuniary burdens it entailed, and through its most critical and important period he was its vital stay and support. It is no figure of speech to aver that in his field of public duty he rendered services not less valuable and splendid than those even of WASHINGTON; though it is necessary to state that he was reimbursed for all his advances.

XXII.

A PROJECT to which Mr. MORRIS attached pre-eminent importance was the erection of a bank. In this the busy, vigorous and capacious mind of ALEXANDER HAMILTON was deeply concerned. Of course there was opposition to it; in good truth, there was opposition to pretty much everything MORRIS undertook to do, though nobody proposed to do better; but his wishes prevailed. Congress, in May 1781, authorized the erection of a bank, and in December passed a formal act incorporating it "for ever," under the name and style of *The President, Directors and Company of the Bank of North America.* The states of Pennsylvania and Massachusetts also granted it charters—more properly the latter chartered a branch—and other states enacted laws for its support and protection in the course of the year 1782. Its capital was fixed at four hundred thousand dollars, with a singular provision to the effect that it should not hold property in value exceeding ten millions of dollars. Subscriptions to the capital were to be paid in gold or silver; and its notes, payable in cash on demand, were to be received in payment of all taxes, duties and debts, due or which might become due to the United States. It began business on the 7th of January 1782, with a subscription aggregating about seventy thousand dollars from private persons [a portion of which were transferred from a former subscription to the Bank of Pennsylvania, of which mention has already been made], and of this small sum not exceeding forty thousand dollars were actually paid in. "I shall do all in my power," said Mr. MORRIS in his Diary under date of January 7th 1782, "to establish and support the bank, and as a beginning have this day drawn my warrant on the treasury for two hundred thousand dollars in part of the shares I have subscribed in behalf of the public." The usefulness of the bank to the government was very great; not so much in the way of direct advances as in the accommodation of persons engaged in supplying the army and in giving stability to the traffic of the community. "The sudden restoration of public and private credit which took place on the establishment of the bank, was an event as extraordinary in itself as any domestic occurrence during the Revolution."[1] An ingenious historian of American Banking Institutions, GOUGE—and joined in this by some others—has endeavoured to discredit the services of the bank, but MORRIS is a better authority: "It may not only be asserted but is demonstrated," he said, "that without the establishment of the national bank, the business of the department of finance could not have been performed,"—for within six months its advances to the government were four hundred and eighty thousand dollars, and up to the 1st of July 1783 its accommodations to government and private persons were over one million.

8. The whole sums received into and paid out of the continental treasury during the years 1781, 1782 and

[1] PAINE: "Dissertations on Government," &c.

1783, made a total of eight millions eight hundred and one thousand seven hundred and ninety-four dollars and sixty-eight cents; that is to say,—

In 1781, . .	$1,942,465.30	
" 1782, . .	3,632,745.85	
" 1783, . .	3,226,583,43—	$8,801,794.68

9. But it must not be supposed, notwithstanding what has been said in a former place concerning the influx of gold and silver into the country in 1780, that the transactions of the treasury were in cash. They were chiefly in bills of credit of Pennsylvania and other states, in the notes issued by the Bank of North America and by ROBERT MORRIS, rated at a specie value; and though the notes signed by Mr. MORRIS were known to be government obligations, the strength of *his* name supported them, and they did not depreciate until near the close of the war, and then only slightly; and ultimately were all redeemed in good faith.[1]

[1] Of the two hundred millions issued by Congress in continental bills of credit, eighty-eight millions received into the state treasuries (at the close of the war) in payment of taxes at the rate of forty for one, had been replaced by bills of the "new tenour," to the amount of four millions four hundred thousand dollars, bearing interest at six per cent. Massachusetts, New Hampshire and Rhode Island had thus taken up and redeemed their entire quotas of the old paper. Connecticut, Delaware, the Carolinas and Georgia had taken up none; the remaining states had taken up and replaced but a part of their quotas. As to the outstanding one hundred and twelve millions there was no thought of redeeming that at any higher rate than seventy-five or one hundred for one. Many of these were in the state treasuries, into which they had come in payment of taxes, but a large amount remained also in the hands of individuals.—HILDRETH iii. 446.

At the time of disbanding the army three months' pay was agreed to be given to the soldiers; and they were allowed to keep their arms and accoutrements as an extra allowance. This pay was to be supplied by the states, but meanwhile was to be advanced from the continental

XXIII.

ON the 30th of October 1781, Congress called upon the states for eight millions of dollars for the service of the war department and the support of the civil establishment in the ensuing year, to be paid in equal quarterly sums, beginning on the 1st of April 1782. On the 4th of September 1782, a call was made for twelve hundred thousand dollars,—"immediately and absolutely necessary for the payment of interest on the public debt;" and six weeks later, October 16th, for a further sum of two millions of dollars, for the service of the year 1783. But in answer to these repeated requisitions, up to the 30th of January 1783, less than fifteen hundred thousand dollars [$1,486,511] had been paid into the continental treasury on account of them! Nor, meantime, was Congress derelict in the adoption of measures—such miserable ones as were in their power—to support and improve the public credit. In February 1781 they recommended the states—as indispensably necessary—to enact laws vesting in Congress "power to levy for the use of the United States a duty of five per cent. ad valorem, at the time and place of importation, upon

treasury in treasury notes,—a new species of paper currency, payable in six months from date, and receivable for all continental taxes. These notes were signed by ROBERT MORRIS, and were finally redeemed out of money borrowed by JOHN ADAMS in Holland in 1784.

all wares, goods and merchandise imported into any of the states from any foreign port, island or plantation, arriving after the 1st of May 1781," excepting, however, certain specified articles; the moneys arising from such duties to be appropriated to the discharge of the principal and interest of the debt already contracted, or which might be contracted on the faith of the United States for the support of the war; and moreover, finally, with power to continue the duties till the debt was fully discharged. Rhode Island utterly refused to comply; Virginia consented, and then retracted her consent, and a third state (Georgia) showed no sign of consciousness of the subject at all. And Congress made a second appeal of a like kind in April 1783, with a substantially similar result.

11. These things being of no avail, the debt remained in a very depraved state. The interest was unpaid, the public credit was as bad as that of the Count Sham Shaller, and the various forms of the debt, being considered of little or no value, were sold by the original holders for an average of about one-tenth their nominal value. The worst of it was, and it *was* a painful business, the army remained unpaid; and in order to prevent some very serious dangers, WASHINGTON, with characteristic caution, separated it as much as he could, and it was discharged without tumult.

XXIV.

THE war was in effect ended by the surrender of CORNWALLIS at Yorktown in October 1781; but it was actually ended by the treaty between the King and the States, concluded in 1782, and officially notified to the American army in April 1783.

Now, it is a subject for wonder, and very great wonder too, that the independence of America was established at all. In the first instance, because a large proportion of the whole people,—certainly one-third of them, and perhaps more nearly a half,—remained loyal to the Crown; many of them went into the British army, to the number of thousands;[1] and they who did not, restrained and embarrassed the efforts of the whigs in a more subtle, but perhaps equally effective way, by discrediting the currency and discouraging in various ways the "sympathizers with the rebellion."

In the second instance, because of that characteristic of the American people which ALEXANDER HAMILTON called "an excess of the spirit of liberty." This was a firm and abiding conviction of the absolute personal and political equality of all the members of the commonwealth. It taught that the judgment of every individual man in the state was equal to that of the

[1] The "loyalists" who served in the British armies from the beginning to the end of the war were not less than 20,000.

whole body of men composing it. Its method of expression was, universal suffrage. The fruits of the doctrine were, pride of personal opinion, and an ineradicable spirit and habit of criticism of those in authority and insubordination against them.[1] Of course among men of this character, the necessarily strict discipline of a regularly organized army was impossible; and it is simply true to say that an effective discipline never did exist among the continental troops. But they were brave and enduring, and fortunately were opposed in the main by troops not much more disciplined than themselves; and they had the incalculable advantage of fighting *for an idea.*

Now, in the third instance, it was a most fortunate circumstance that WASHINGTON was known to be unambitious, and that he was not the possessor of a brilliant and daring genius, but that he did carry in himself those noble qualities which beget among men solid convictions of respect and confidence. He cared nothing for political honours; still less was he ambitious of a crown; he was not an overshadowing image, save in moral qualities, and his conduct of the war was cautious and careful, rather than enterprising and splendid. Wherefore he was satisfactory to his compatriots. He escaped the jealousies and suspicions which a man of vigorous action would have excited; though he did not wholly avoid imputation. It is no

---

[1] How far universal suffrage, and the natural necessary consequences which flow from a universal participation by all citizens in the political power of the state, are *hostile* to the effective discipline of armies, is an inquiry well worthy the careful examination of political philosophers.

matter of doubt at all that WASHINGTON alone, of all the men of his time, was fitted for the leadership, and that but for WASHINGTON, the revolution would have failed at the end of the third year of the struggle, if not sooner.

In the fourth instance, the weakness of the continental Congress clogged the conduct of the war at almost every step. Perhaps in all history there never was a body at once so powerful and so helpless as this. It exercised all the powers of the national sovereignty, and yet never collected a dollar of taxes in its own right. It accredited its ministers to foreign courts, and received ambassadors in return, but would have trembled to appoint a tax-collector in Rhode Island or Delaware. It created armies, emitted money, made foreign loans, and had no certain resources upon which to base any one of those acts. In a word, it was a sovereign and a mendicant.

In the fifth instance, because of the disorganization and inefficiency of the state governments, and of the jealousies existing between them. There was a good deal of fear that some one of them would do more than its share, and that some others would do less; while lethargy, and inability, and "states' rights," all entered in to make up the whole sum of the public difficulties.

In the sixth instance, because of the extensive financial disorders and embarrassments which have been but imperfectly detailed in these pages. In the early years of the war, incompetent, inefficient and wasteful administration; in the later years, biting, pinching *poverty*—that poverty which ROBERT BURNS has called the "half-sister of death and the cousin-german of hell."[1]

It is, after all, to FRANCE—our most glorious and noble ally, the first of the nations of modern Europe notwithstanding her recent great defeat, and grander and more admirable in adversity than in victory,—it is to FRANCE as much as to ourselves that the American people owe their deliverance from the British Crown. It was because of the French alliance that Spain and Holland were embroiled in war with England; it was because England was at war with France and Spain and Holland, that she was effectually prevented from putting forth, upon American soil, all her immense energies toward "crushing the rebellion," and was finally forced to acknowledge the thirteen colonies as FREE AND INDEPENDENT STATES. And of all the political events of modern history, the admission of American independence has been the weightiest in its effect upon the destinies of mankind; whether for good or for evil, men will be better prepared to speak a century hence.

CALONNE stated in 1786 that the cost of the American war to France had been fourteen hundred and forty millions of francs, or two hundred and fifty-six millions of dollars,—a vast sum, and one showing the extent of the French efforts. The English national debt was increased by the war from £123,000,000 at its beginning to £238,000,000 at its close; in dollars about five hundred and seventy-five millions, besides actual payments on account of it drawn from taxes.

---

[1] "Poverty! thou half-sister of death, thou cousin-german of hell, where shall I find force of execration equal to the aptitude of thy demerits?"—BURNS.

XXV.

THE condition of the public finances on the 1st of January 1783 was thus stated:—

Due to the Farmers-General of France . . .	1,000,000 livres.
Due to individuals in France in unliquidated accounts estimated	3,000,000 "
Due to the Crown of France, including a loan of 10,000,000 borrowed in Holland, guaranteed by France	28,000,000 "
Due to Crown of France, loan	6,000,000 "
	38,000,000 "

Translated into dollars at five livres eight sous per dollar .	$7,037,037
Due to lenders in Holland, received in part of the loan contracted by John Adams, 1,678,000 florins	671,200
Borrowed in Spain by John Jay	150,000
One year's interest on Dutch loan	26,848
Whole foreign debt	$7,885,085

Loan-office certificates reduced to cash value . . .	$11,463,802
Interest unpaid 1781	190,000
" " 1782	687,828
Credit to sundries in treasury books	638,042
Army debt to 31st December 1782	5,635,618
Unliquidated debt estimated at	8,000,000
Commutation to the army[1]	5,000,000
Bounty due to privates	500,000
Deficiencies in 1783 supposed to be	2,000,000
	34,115,290
	7,885,085
Whole debts	$42,000,375
Add total of arrears on both foreign and domestic debt, on account of interest	$2,415,956

[1] The half-pay establishment was adopted to the great offence of some

2. In addition to these debts of the confederation, were those of the individual states, which at the close

---

of the states, and these sent petitions to Congress against the measure, representing it as impolitic and unjust. In addition to the allowances of Congress, the states generally made provision for their own lines. In Pennsylvania, for example, the depreciation of pay was fully made up; at the sales of confiscated estates their certificates were received the same as if they were hard money; they were received at a hard-money value at the land offices; the interest on their certificates was for several years paid; an additional bounty of land was given to them, ready surveyed and free from expense, and when the public debt was funded (by the United States) their three per cent. and deferred debt were made good by additional certificates from the state, which were afterwards redeemed at from fifty to thirty per cent. in hard money.—In December 1782 a deputation of officers waited upon Congress and presented a strong memorial from the army touching their sufferings, and asked Congress, first, *for some present pay;* secondly, *for a settlement of their accounts and security for the balances;* and thirdly, *for a commutation of their half-pay for life,*—as they found that that measure was odious to their fellow-citizens, and would prevent the happy intercourse they expected when they returned to private life. Some present pay and a settlement of accounts were immediately provided for, and as to security for the balances, Congress resolved that for whatever was found due on settlement, the troops of the United States had an undoubted right to expect such security, and that every effort in their power should be made to obtain from the states substantial funds adequate to the object. Touching the matter of the commutation, it was represented on the part of the army that five or six years' full pay was but a reasonable compensation, not only on account of the deficiency in pay but on other accounts; and that it would be more agreeable to the feelings of the people than that they should be pensioners for life, and they were willing to receive the commutation in certificates of debt of the United States--there being no money indeed—the same as other public creditors. It was finally determined to accede to this, but in order to prevent the officers from alienating their certificates at an under rate, and so injuring the public credit, it was proposed to make the commutation certificates non-transferable. Whereupon the deputation asked if they were not freemen, and whether they had not the same right to dispose of their property as other citizens? which Congress could not gainsay, and on the 22d of March 1783 resolved that the half-pay for life should be commuted, and that the officers entitled to it should receive instead of half-pay the sum of five years' full pay, in money or securities of the of the war amounted to about twenty millions of dollars. Of these, in some of the states small parts were paid interim between the end of the war and the establishment of the government of the United States, when they were assumed by the Union and fixed at an aggregate of $21,500,000.

3. The whole expenses of the war were never ascertained of course; and they have been estimated at various amounts. THOMAS JEFFERSON'S estimate was $170,000,000; that of Mr. GERRY is no doubt nearer the truth; his estimate was $180,000,000. In 1790 the Register of the Treasury stated the cash expenditures of the continental treasury at $92,485,693.15, as follows:—

1775, 1776	at specie value	$20,064,566.66
1777	" "	24,986,646.85
1778	" "	24,289,438.26
1779	" "	10,794,620.65
1780	" "	3,000,000.00
1781	" "	1,942,465.30
1782	" "	3,632,745.85
1783	" "	3,226,583.43
1784 (to Nov. 1st)		548,525.03
	Total	$92,485,693.15
To these cash disbursements were to be added arrears on account of army pay, foreign expenditures and the state debts (assumed at $21,500,000)		42,708,009.75
	Total	$135,193,703.00

United States at six per cent. per annum, as Congress should find most convenient, though it was left at the option of the lines of the respective states either to accept or decline the commutation,—which amounted to $4500 to a colonel, and $2400 to a captain. This commutation system, however, was scarcely less offensive to many of the people than the half-pay establishment itself.

In this estimate of the Register are not included the actual expenditures of the states, exclusive of their debts. Their total emissions of bills of credit aggregated two hundred millions (and these mainly shared the fate of the continental bills), worth, at the several periods of their issue, thirty-five millions; they drew in by taxes, say, six millions more,—total, forty-one millions. But to these sums ought to be added the natural necessary waste of the war by destruction of buildings and crops, and the large subsistence of troops on both sides by forced levies, and the contributions of private persons and associations; certainly not less in the aggregate than ten millions,—making a grand total of one hundred and eighty-six millions.

4. But whether this sum represents the actual cost of the war may well be doubted, for it seems to be pretty clear that the issues of continental bills of credit were materially in excess of the emissions authorized by Congress. There were paid out of the continental treasury of old and new emissions during the six years the war was conducted upon paper, of the former $357,476,641 and of the latter $2,070,485—total, $359,547,126. There were authorized of the former $200,000,000 and of the latter $10,000,000. There were received into the treasury from all sources, that is to say—

From old emissions authorized	$200,000,000
From new emissions actually paid in	2,070,485
From all other sources, including loans	63,289,212
	$265,359,697
From emissions authorized to replace mutilated bills[1]	25,552,780
From emissions authorized to replace counterfeited bills	10,000,000
	$300,912,477

[1] Statement of Thomas Jefferson.

The result therefore is,—Received into the treasury from all sources, $300,912,477; paid out on all accounts, $359,547,126,—excess of disbursements over receipts, $58,634,649.

5. Now, interim between the peace and the inauguration of the Federal government, Congress had no means of paying either principal or interest of the debt, except by requisitions upon the states, and they had no power to enforce them of course; so that all their efforts were vain. Though during the years 1782, '84, '85, and '86 requisitions—for payment of interest—were made amounting in the aggregate to $6,279,376, up to the 31st of March 1787 but one million ($1,003,725) had been paid into the continental treasury, leaving a balance due of $5,275,650.

6. But, after all, the condition of Congress was no worse than that of the states and the private people. During the war, or at any rate the latter years of it, the collection of debts was widely suspended, and on the return of peace a flood of foreign products were poured into the country, much beyond the means of payment of the importers, though they drained the states of their coin; then came more bills of credit and severe tender laws to support them; the upshot of the whole business being that the people could not pay their debts, and the courts were filled with plaintiffs and defendants, and that the states, suffering from the prevailing disorders, had more than they could do to provide for their own internal administration and the payment of their own debts, which they didn't pay either. But a more serious difficulty was the jealousies arising between the importing and the non-

importing states. The former, having convenient ports, found it to their advantage to raise money by duties on imported merchandises, while they who received their foreign goods through this means were indignant and unhappy about it, and averred that they had only changed masters, and that instead of being taxed by the British Parliament, they were taxed by neighbouring states; and doubtless a good many of this complaining sort of people would have preferred the old masters to the new. Briefly, then, trade was obstructed, industry decayed and hard times on all sides; and everybody began to see that a remedy must be applied, or that the fruits of the war would be lost through internal dissensions and not impossibly through internal wars.

7. All of which resulted in a convention of delegates from the several states, who met to consider the public disorders and devise remedies for them. These framed *the Constitution,* which being submitted to the people or the states—nobody seems to know exactly which—they, the people or the states, or both, after a great deal of debate and dispute, finally ratified it, and it became in theory at least—for no merely written instrument can ever become so in reality—the supreme law of the American Union. It contained one important provision bearing upon this history: it declared that all the debts and engagements contracted by the confederated states should be valid as against the United States.

XXVI.

It remains to show the mode in which the war debts of the Revolution were finally settled and discharged.

2. The government of the United States was organized by the inauguration of President Washington at New York, April 30th 1789. The treasury department was established by the act of September 2d subsequent, and on the 11th of September Alexander Hamilton was appointed Secretary. On the 9th of January 1790 Mr. Hamilton informed the House of Representatives of his readiness to submit plans for the support of public credit. This notice gave instant rise to a somewhat excited debate touching the mode in which the Secretary should communicate with the House,—whether by written report or oral statement. The unreasoning terror of monarchy[1] which in those days prevailed among all classes and conditions of Americans, triumphed over what would seem to be

---

[1] During and since the war of the rebellion, efforts have been made to change the law, so that the Secretary of the Treasury may personally appear in the House of Representatives and explain his "budget" and his plans. But the prejudices of revolutionary times, in this matter of real importance, seem still to reign paramount.

the good sense of the thing, and he was directed to report in writing, which he accordingly did.

3. In that important paper the Secretary carefully reviewed the origin of the debt and the terms upon which it had been contracted, and elaborately argued the methods by which he proposed its payment should be effected. Touching the foreign debt, no difference of opinion existed, either in Congress or out, as to the precise obligations it involved. It was quite otherwise with respect to the domestic debt. That was already the subject of a virulent excitement and controversy; and it had been strenuously insisted by a large party in the country—headed in Congress by Mr. MADISON—that there ought to be a discrimination between the original holders and the present possessors by purchase. Mr. HAMILTON combated these views with vigorous and invincible arguments, and declared that such a discrimination would be unjust, impolitic, highly injurious even to the original holders, and ruinous to the public credit. The project of discrimination was after a long debate rejected. But a second question, and one of far greater importance, arose upon a proposal that the debts of the individual states should be assumed by the United States. It was debated with great feeling and vehemence; the excitement spread throughout the country, and reached a pitch of anger and violence which seriously threatened the stability of the Union. "This is a measure," said an eminent leader in the opposition, "which has not only agitated Congress, but it has more or less convulsed the whole people of the United States. It has elated speculators

and state brokers, while it has depressed three-fourths of the honest part of the community. It has held out alluring prospects of fortune to the one, while it has blasted and withered the just expectations of the other. It has been the centre-pin of visionary projectors, but its future effects are viewed with horror by disinterested men." But HAMILTON urged the measure upon the score alike of policy and justice. A provision for the state debts emanating from one authority, he asserted, would be more effectual than when coming from several authorities, and the revenue required in either case would be the same. Collision and confusion would be prevented, and the public creditors receiving their dues from a single source, distributed with an equal hand, would have a common interest in supporting the fiscal arrangements of the government. It was hence the interest of the creditors of the Union "that those of the states should be comprehended in a general provision. Neither would it be just that one class of public creditors should be more favoured than the other. The objects for which both debts were contracted were the same; indeed, a great part of the state debts had arisen from assumptions by them on account of the Union." But however just these views of Mr. HAMILTON, the rock of the national resources would *not* have responded to his touch but for the intervention of THOMAS JEFFERSON, who—being by nature and habit an intriguer—brought about a compromise which resulted in the substantial adoption of HAMILTON'S plans.

4. With respect to the arrears of interest, HAMILTON

contended that they were entitled to an equal provision with the principal of the debt.

5. He considered the whole debt in the light of an annuity, bearing interest at the rate of six per cent. per annum, redeemable at the option of the government upon payment of the principal; and proposed five different plans of loans to be at the election of the creditor. The first of these proposed to pay the creditor one-third of his claim in western lands. With respect to the foreign debt, the Secretary was of opinion that it ought to be paid with new loans obtained abroad; and for the payment of interest and the current service of government, he thought additional duties might be laid on wines, spirits, teas and coffees. And while he was persuaded that the proper funding of the existing debt would render it a national blessing, yet he was far from acceding to the position, in the latitude in which it was sometimes laid down, that "public debts are public benefits,"—a position inviting to prodigality and liable to dangerous abuse,—and he ardently wished it established as a fundamental maxim in the system of public credit of the United States, *that the creation of debt should always be accompanied with the means of extinguishment.* He regarded this as the true secret for rendering public credit immortal. He proposed, therefore, that the net product of the post-office establishment to an amount not exceeding one million of dollars yearly should be vested in commissioners, to be applied by them to the discharge of the public debt until the whole should be paid.

6. He thus stated the debt as it then existed :—

The Foreign Debt.

Amount of the principal	$10,070,307.00
Arrears of interest to 31st December 1789 . . .	1,640,071.62
Making together	$11,710,378.62

The Domestic Debt.

Principal of the liquidated part	$27,383,917.74
Arrears of interest to 31st December 1790 . . .	13,030,168.20
Making together	$40,144,085.94
The unliquidated part of the domestic debt, which consists chiefly of continental bills of credit, not ascertained but estimated at	$2,000,000.00
These several sums constituting the whole debt . .	$54,124,464.56
The debts of the individual states were not ascertained, but they were estimated by the Secretary, principal and interest, at	$25,000,000.00
Whole estimated amount of debt . .	$79,124,464.56

7. The Secretary said also that he contemplated the erection of a NATIONAL BANK,[1] for which, with the permission of the House, he would submit a plan in the course of the session.

[1] Mr. HAMILTON submitted his plan for a national bank, as he threatened to do, December 13th 1790; and *it* also excited a virulent debate, in the course of which Mr. MADISON made his celebrated speech discussing the doctrine of "implied powers." THOMAS JEFFERSON opposed it with great bitterness; but the bank was authorized by the act of February 25th 1791, under the name and style of "The President, Directors and Company of the Bank of the United States." The capital was fixed at ten millions of dollars, and the President was authorized to subscribe towards the said capital, on behalf of the United States, not exceeding two millions; and the bills or notes of the bank, payable in gold or silver on demand, were to be receivable in payment of all dues to the government. Its privileges were to cease on the 4th of March 1811. Like all of HAMILTON's bills prepared for the action of Congress, this one also contained a preamble, which alleged, among other things, that the bank would be "conducive to the successful conducting of the national finances, and tend to give facility to the obtaining of loans for

XXVII.

THE act of Congress, approved March 4th 1790, begins with a preamble which recites that "justice and the support of the public credit require that pro-

---

the use of the government in sudden emergencies," besides being productive of advantage to trade and industry in general.

Here are words of wisdom from HAMILTON's report on a national bank, which may serve to moderate the enthusiasm of some of those paper money advocates who "imagine vain things" of that profound and most admirable statesman.

The emitting of paper money, he says, by the authority of government is wisely prohibited to the individual states by the national constitution; and the spirit of that prohibition ought not to be disregarded by the government of the United States. Though paper emissions under a general authority might have some advantages not applicable, and be free from some disadvantages which are applicable to the like emissions by the states separately, yet they are of a nature so liable to abuse—and, it may even be affirmed, so certain of being abused—that the wisdom of the government will be shown in never trusting itself with the use of so seducing and dangerous an expedient. In times of tranquillity it might have no ill consequence; it might even perhaps be managed in a way to be productive of good, but in great and trying emergencies there is almost a moral certainty of its becoming mischievous. The stamping of paper is an operation so much easier than the laying of taxes, that a government in the practice of paper emissions would rarely fail, in any emergency, to indulge itself too far in the employment of that resource to avoid, as much as possible, one less auspicious to present popularity. If it should not even be carried so far as to be rendered an absolute bubble, it would at least be likely to be extended to a degree which would occasion an inflated and artificial state of things, incompatible with the regular and prosperous course of the political economy.—[ALEXANDER HAMILTON's Report on a National Bank, communicated to the House of Representatives December 13th 1790.]

vision should be made for fulfilling the engagements of the United States, in respect of their foreign debt, and for funding their domestic debt upon equitable and satisfactory terms." And accordingly provision is thus made:

2. After reserving out of the yearly income of the customs and tonnage duties six hundred thousand dollars, for the support of the government of the United States and "their common defence," the residue of the funds so derived were appropriated to the payment of the interest on the foreign loans already made or which might be made in the future, and the whole or any part of the principal of the debt; and the President was authorized "to cause to be borrowed" not exceeding twelve millions of dollars, so much of which as was necessary to the purpose to be devoted to the payment of the arrears of interest on the foreign debt, and the remainder to the discharge of the principal. But the President was not to make any contract or engagement which should preclude the United States from reimbursing any sums borrowed under this authority within fifteen years.

3. And a loan of the full amount of the domestic debt was also authorized; and in payment of subscriptions thereto the commissioners of loans were authorized to receive the various certificates which had been issued on account of the continental debt, including the bills of credit at the rate of one hundred dollars in bills for one in cash. The interest on this portion of the debt was fixed at six per cent., and the principal was subject to redemption at the election of the government, in payments not exceeding in one year,

on account of both principal and interest, the proportion of eight dollars upon every hundred; but upon one-third of the debt, or thirty-three and one-third dollars in each hundred, the payment of interest did not begin until the year 1800. The interest on subscriptions paid in "indents of interest" was fixed at three per cent. per annum, and the principal was to be redeemable at any time at the election of the government.

4. The debts authorized to be assumed on account of the several states were as follows: New Hampshire, three hundred thousand dollars; Massachusetts, four millions of dollars; Rhode Island, two hundred thousand dollars; Connecticut, one million six hundred thousand dollars; New York, one million two hundred thousand dollars; New Jersey, eight hundred thousand dollars; Pennsylvania, two million two hundred thousand dollars; Delaware, two hundred thousand dollars; Maryland, eight hundred thousand dollars; Virginia, three million five hundred thousand dollars; North Carolina, two million four hundred thousand dollars; South Carolina, four millions of dollars; and Georgia, three hundred thousand dollars.[1]

5. And the faith of the United States was pledged to provide and appropriate permanent funds for the payment of the interest on the stocks created in pursuance of the act.

6. The total debt of the United States on the 1st of January 1791 was—

[1] The sum of the state debts to be assumed by the United States was estimated by Hamilton at $21,500,000; the sum actually assumed was $18,328,186.21.

1. *Foreign debt*	$12,812,831.92
2. *Domestic debt*	
Six per cent. and deferred stocks	1,143,106.28
Three per cent. stock	425,911.33
Unfunded debt	61,081,626.99
Making altogether	$75,463,476.52
But deduct payments on account of subsequent years to amount of	293,502.31
Actual total of debt	$75,169,974.21

The foreign debt was due, $7,561,449.42 to France; $250,382.50 to Spain; and $5,001,000.00 to Holland.

7. Between 1791 and 1795, and including those years, the debt due to France was discharged with moneys borrowed in Holland, as was also that due to Spain, which was paid in 1792 and 1793. The whole foreign debt on the 1st of January 1796 was $11,939,000, and bore interest at four and four and one-half per centum per annum; was wholly due in Holland; and was finally extinguished in the year 1810.

XXVIII.

WITH respect to the domestic debt of the United States, a fund was created for its redemption, which was placed under the management of the Vice-President, the Chief Justice of the Supreme Court, the Secretary of State, the Secretary of the Treasury and the Attorney-General, who were constituted the "Commissioners of the Sinking Fund." This was by act of Congress August 12th 1790. In March 1795 an act was passed making further provision for the redemption of the debt. It provided for the creation of a fund out of certain specified branches of the revenues of the government, which was pledged inviolably to remain and be appropriated and vested in the Commissioners of the Sinking Fund as "property in trust," until the whole debt should be fully and completely paid; and all priorities before established with respect to the different portions of it were to cease unless the creditor signified his dissent in writing,—so that the whole sums appropriated towards the payment of the debt should constitute a common fund, chargeable without distinction for the benefit of all the public creditors.

2. Payments on account of the debt were steadily made, and it was constantly reduced in amount until, on the 1st of January 1812, its total was but $45,035,-

123.70, and was inclusive of fifteen millions borrowed in 1803[1] to pay the Louisiana purchase. The war of 1812 added largely to the debt; on the 1st of January 1816 it was $123,016,375; on the 30th September 1820 it was stated at $91,225.560, of which sum $20,570,627 was of the debt contracted before the year 1812.

3. "If Providence permits me to meet you in another session," said President JACKSON in his message of December 1833, "I shall have the high gratification of announcing to you that the national debt is extinguished. I cannot refrain from expressing the pleasure I feel at the near approach of that desirable event. The short period of time within which the public debt will have been discharged is strong evidence of the abundant resources of the country, and of the prudence and economy with which the government has heretofore been administered. We have waged two wars since we became a nation, with one of the most powerful kingdoms in the world; both of them undertaken in defence of our dearest rights — both successfully prosecuted and honourably terminated; and many of those who partook in the first struggle, as well as the second, will have lived to see the last item of the debt incurred in those necessary but expensive conflicts faithfully and honestly discharged; and we shall have the proud satisfaction of bequeathing to the public servants who follow us in the administration of the government, the rare blessing of a revenue sufficiently

[1] At this time $38,035,564 of the debt was held in the United States and $32,119,210 in foreign countries. The number of stockholders in the United States was 14,236.

abundant, raised without injustice or oppression to our citizens, and unencumbered with any burdens but what they themselves shall think proper to impose upon it."

4. In his message to Congress December 7th 1835, President JACKSON announced that the debt had been finally redeemed, and added that it was expected that at the close of the current year there would remain in the treasury an unappropriated balance of nearly eleven millions of dollars.

A.

A TABLE

Showing the amount of Bills of Credit authorized by the Continental Congress during the War of the Revolution. Communicated to the House of Representatives, January 30th, 1828, by JOSEPH NOURSE, Register of the Treasury.

Date of Congressional Resolve.		*Vol.*	*Page.*	*Amount authorized.*
1775.	June 22,	1	125	$2,000,000
	July 25,	1	177	1,000,000
	November 29,	1	273	3,000,000
1776.	February 17,	2	66	4,000,000
	May 9 and 27,	2	164	5,000,000
	July 22 and Aug. 13,	2	280, 308	5,000,000
	Nov. 2 and Dec. 28,	2	440, 509	5,000,000
1777.	February 26,	3	80	5,000,000
	May 20,	3	194	5,000,000
	August 15,	3	331	1,000,000
	November 7,	3	480	1,000,000
	December 3,	3	555	1,000,000
1778.	January 8,	4	12	1,000,000
	January 22,	4	47	2,000,000
	February 16,	4	101	2,000,000
	March 5,	4	133	2,000,000
	April 4,	4	190	1,000,000
	April 11,	4	209	5,000,000
	April 18,	4	223	500,000
	May 22,	4	303	5,000,000
	June 20,	4	362	5,000,009
	July 30,	4	434	5,000,000
	September 5,	4	521	5,000,000
	September 26,	4	567	10,000,000
	November 4,	4	639	10,000,000
	December 14,	4	713	10,000,000
1779.	February 3,	5	43	5,000,160
	February 19,	5	64	5,000,160
	April 1,	5	132	5,000,160
	May 5,	5	183	10,000,100
	January 4 and May 7,	5	84, 188	50,000,100
	June 4,	5	240	10,000,100
	July 17,	5	288	5,000,180
	July 17,	5	289	10,000,100
	September 17,	5	360	5,000,180
	September 17,	5	360	10,000,180
	October 14,	5	384	5,000,180
	November 17,	5	419	5,000,040
	November 17,	5	420	5,050,500
	November 29,	5	438	10,000,140
				$241,552,780

B.

THOMAS JEFFERSON'S TABLE.

Date of Authority.		*Sum emitted.*	*Depreciation.*	*Cash value.*
1775.	June 23,	$2,000,000		$2,000,000
	November 29,	3,000,000		3,000,000
1776.	February 17,	4,000,000		4,000,000
	August 13,	5,000,000		5,000,000
1777.	May 20,	5,000,000	2, 2, 3	1,877,273
	August 15,	1,000,000	3	333,333⅓
	November 7,	1,000,000	4	250,000
	December 3,	1,000,000	4	250,000
1778.	January 8,	1,000,000	4	250,000
	January 22,	2,000,000	4	500,000
	February 16,	2,000,000	5	400,000
	March 5,	2,000,000	5	400,000
	April 4,	1,000,000	6	166,666⅔
	April 11,	5,000,000	6	833,333⅓
	April 18,	500,000	6	88,333⅓
	May 22,	5,000,000	5	1,000,000
	June 20,	5,000,000	4	1,250,000
	July 30,	5,000,000	4½	1,111,111
	September 5,	5,000,000	5	1,000,000
	September 26,	10,000,100	5	2,000,020
	November 4,	10,000,100	3	1,666,683⅓
	December 14	10,000,100	6	1,666,683⅓
1779.	January 14,	[1]24,447,620	8	3,055,952½
	Febrbary 3,	5,000,160	10	500,016
	February 12,	5,000,160	10	500,016
	April 2,	5,000,160	17	294,127
	May 5,	10,000,100	24	416,670⅚
	June 4,	10,009,100	20	500,005
	June 17,	15,000,280	20	750,014
	September 17,	15,000,260	24	625,010⅚
	October 14,	5,000,180	30	166,672⅔
	November 17,	10,050,540	38½	261,053
	November 29,	10,000,140	38½	259,743
		$200,000,000		$36,367,719⅚

(1) The sum actually voted was $50,000,400, but part of it was for exchange of old bills, without saying how much. It is presumed that these exchanges absorbed $25,552,780, because $24,447,620, with all the other emissions preceding September 2d, 1779, will amount to $159,-948,880, the sum which Congress declared to be then in circulation.

C.—TABLE OF ISSUES BY THE SEVERAL COLONIES.

	1775.	1776.	1777.	1778.	1779.	1780.	1781.	1783.	TOTALS.
Massachusetts,									$3,868,000
Rhode Island,	$200,000	$300,000	$15,000		$133,000	$66,600			714,600
Connecticut,	500,000	366,300	17,500			632,700			1,516,500
New York,	112,500	637,500					$411,250		1,161,250
New Jersey,		133,000				600,000	800,000	$85,000	1,618,000
Pennsylvania,	420,000	227,000	532,000			1,516,000	1,330,000	300,000	4,325,000
Delaware,	80,000		66,500						146,500
Maryland,	535,111	415,111							950,000
Virginia,	875,000	1,500,000	2,700,000	2,700,000	2,500,000	30,666,000	87,500,000		128,441,000
North Carolina,				2,125,000	1,250,000	3,600,000	26,250,000	100,000	33,325,000
South Carolina,									33,458,926
									$209,524,776
Congress,									241,552,380
								Total issues authorized,	$451,077,156

NOTE.—The foregoing table, though not containing *all* the issues authorized by the colonies during the years named (there seems to have been *none* authorized in 1782), is as complete as I have been able to make it, with such means of information as have been accessible to me. It is approximately correct.

D.

A TABLE OF THE DEPRECIATION OF CONTINENTAL BILLS.

COMPILED FROM MERCHANTS' BOOKS AT PHILADELPHIA.

	1777	1778	1779	1780	1781
January,	1¼	4	7, 8, 9	40, 45	100
February,	1½	5	10	45, 55	100, 120
March,	2	5	10, 11	60, 65	120, 135
April,	2½	6	12½, 16, 14, 22	60	135, 200
May,	2½	5	22, 24	60	200, 500
June,	2½	4	22, 20, 18	69	
July,	3	4	18, 19, 20	60, 65	
August,	3	6	20	65, 75	
September,	3	5	20, 28	75	
October,	3	5	30	75, 80	
November,	3	6	32, 45	80, 100	
December,	4	6	45, 38	100	